BUT WHERE
DO I PUT
the couch?

Melissa Michaels
The Inspired Room

KariAnne Wood
Thistlewood Farms

HARVEST HOUSE PUBLISHERS
EUGENE, OREGON

But where do I put the couch?

Right? How many of us have looked at a room and asked that question? *A lot.*

We know because during our 20-plus years of combined blogging, that question has surfaced more often than a lint-covered quarter from beneath a sofa cushion. We wrote this book to answer *those* questions—the ones we all face in moments of desperation or creative burnout. To keep it real, these questions are gathered from our blog followers who are now eager for answers. And here they are! So sit back, relax, and get ready to resolve a few home décor conundrums.

And along the way, you will find the perfect place for that couch.

Melissa & KariAnne

CONTENTS

Getting Started

How do I start when I don't know where to start? Whether you're refinishing a table or furnishing an entire home, often the hardest part of decorating is the whole getting started process. Maybe you have a distinct vision of what you want, but you don't have the budget or can't find the pieces to make it work. Maybe your home is hopelessly out of date and you're completely lost as to where to begin. Or maybe you've collected pieces you love and have a Pinterest board full of inspiration, but you're terrified to take that first step.

You got this, friend.

Truly.

The secret to getting started is...*getting started.* Even when you feel a little overwhelmed and are second-guessing your decorating decisions. Getting started is where it's at. That's really the only solution. There isn't a tried-and-true method for decorating—only what works for *you.* Once you take that first step, once you begin, once you follow your heart and step out in faith, you are well on your way to turning your decorating dreams into reality.

1

But Where Do
I Put the Couch?

Help! I really want to turn my house into a home, but I have no idea where to start! I'm not even sure where to put the couch! I keep staring at my living room and I'm stumped. Is there a rule I should follow? Or maybe I just need the confidence to try something unexpected. Can you help?

Kathleen M.

Melissa & KariAnne say...

Whether you're staring at a wide-open, empty space or have embraced the same decorating scheme for decades, knowing where to start decorating or redecorating can be intimidating. What if you choose the wrong style? What if things don't end up matching well? What if you put the couch in the wrong place and the room just doesn't make sense?

Truth? Every room can throw you a curve ball—or an angled wall! But don't worry. We've both stood in your shoes (or slippers), overwhelmed with furniture placement and unsure of where exactly to set that sofa.

Perhaps you've had your couch in the same place for ten or more years and have always assumed that's where it goes. But now? You want to redo and rearrange and get a new look. Or you're starting from scratch with an empty room. You've moved the couch from wall to wall, but you just can't decide on the perfect place. And no matter where you place it, it's hard to envision the rest of the room.

Here are some suggestions to help you get past this decorating hurdle:

- **Start by finding the focal point of a room.** Determine your focal point by following your eye. What draws your attention when you walk into the room? In many cases, this is the fireplace or mantel. It could also be a large picture window with an incredible view or an oversized painting. Place the couch facing the wall with the focal point. Next, add chairs, side tables, and other furniture and accessories based on your couch's location in the room. Your focal point is now center stage in your space.

- **If you have a larger room with two sofas, keep the furniture arrangement symmetrical.** Arrange the sofas across from each other. You want the bigger pieces in a room to be visually balanced, and arranging them in this manner is the best way to achieve that balance. (Note: It's best if the sofas match each other.

If they're not the same, tie them together with coordinating pillow colors and patterns, as well as cozy throw blankets.)

- **It's generally not a good idea to block a window.** But if you have a lower sofa and a big window, consider placing the sofa in front of that wall.

- **Resist the urge to shove the sofa against a wall.** Depending on how much room you have available, try "floating" the sofa (as well as the other furniture) in the room. Ideally, you want to place your furniture about 12" from the wall. Moving the furniture into the room creates cozier spaces and helps with traffic flow. You can also add items of interest behind the sofa—a potted plant, an attractive floor lamp, a small shelf, or a narrow sofa table.

- **Get creative with sectionals.** Often it's assumed the natural placement for a sectional is in the corner of a room, but instead, try pulling it away from the walls. With a sectional, you have a ton of seating space available, so you don't need as many other pieces for seating in the room. This gives you the freedom to try some creative layouts.

- **Improve a box-shaped room.** Got a space lacking details (such as built-ins, chair rails, or coved ceilings)? Perhaps your furniture arrangement could shake things up and provide some interest. Try putting a small sofa or chair at a 45-degree angle. You might even try angling your rug. Why not? The key is to keep trying different arrangements until you hit on a solution that seems creative yet functional.

- **In a larger room, it's important to create conversation circles.** If all the furniture is pushed against the walls, it can be challenging to communicate across the distance. Try floating a sofa (or even two sofas facing each other) around a coffee table along with chairs set in the circle to close up any gaps.

Don't worry if none of these solutions work for you, or if you make one choice about where to put your sofa and then six weeks later you decide you want to do something different. Our best decorating advice of all? Do what makes you happy—including deciding where to put your couch. Step back, look at the room, and let go of perfection. Because here's the thing: There may not be a perfect location for your couch. It may take trial and error (or trying your couch in several different locations) to finally land on an arrangement that works best for you. The room may not be perfect, but it can be comfortable. Designing your home is about serving your family's needs and making the people who live there feel at home.

As you read through the rest of the decorating questions and answers in this book, we want you to keep that in mind. We'll offer you our very best advice and be cheering you on, but we believe that ultimately you are the best judge of what will work for you in your home.

So don't feel intimidated by rules, limitations, or possibilities. You've got this! Truly. Your new design is going to be as amazing as you are.

2

Which Big Projects Should I Do First?

I have a decorating plan for my home, but how do I know where to begin with the big projects, especially when my life is so busy? I've always wondered about the best sequence to follow. For example, do I paint the walls before or after I put in new flooring?

Peggy L.

Melissa says...

How you update your important backdrops—floors and walls—can be one of the most influential decorating choices and investments you will make. To get the most out of this big step, I suggest you start right where you are standing! Between the two, floors are the more permanent design element, so you can save money, effort, and potential frustration if you first select and install the floor tones and textures that make your heart skip a beat. Once this new foundation becomes a part of the visual flow of a room or area of your house, then you'll have confidence to choose the wall treatment.

Following this sequence has great benefits. Flooring will literally set the tone of a space. If you installed a warm, honey-hued floor, the cooler blue wall color that caught your eye six months ago in a magazine might not feel as complementary as you'd like. If you have the luxury of time, give yourself a month to live with the new flooring and then make the final paint choice. (And before a roller spreads the cheer of a new color, be sure to protect that new foundation with sturdy plastic or canvas.)

Chances are, other décor choices will cause you to hesitate. If so, you're not alone. In fact, the membership of the

"How do I make decorating progress without losing my mind?" club is growing exponentially.

As a blogger, I receive a lot of questions from readers asking how I get everything done in life and accomplish my decorating projects. But here's the truth: Just like you, my life is busy with family and friends and work and obligations, and I have to pace myself and prioritize.

A popular time-management principle is illustrated by filling a jar with rocks and sand. You want to put the rocks in the jar first (which represent your big projects) and then add the sand (the little projects). This is a great analogy for beginning the decorating process in your home. To reverse the method—sand before rocks—would be inefficient and frustrating.

If the talk of sand makes you want to procrastinate even longer by purchasing a flight to Hawaii THIS MINUTE, then let me help you another way. When I have a big project that needs to get done, I give myself permission to START the project even though I fear I'm too busy to FINISH it anytime soon. It makes sense to do the big, messy stuff first, even though it's tempting to begin with a smaller project that will take less time to complete. But I think starting a project and being in *process* is better than never getting around to anything.

Sure, it can be inconvenient and disruptive—but eventually it's going to get done. I still invite guests over for dinner. The kids are still allowed to have friends visit. Bible studies and book groups can still meet regularly in our home. Paint cans and ladders are just part of the temporary décor, and most people don't seem to mind.

While I wish I had the luxury of a whole week off to paint my house or refinish my kitchen cabinets, I can't reserve that kind of time for home transformations. I have to accept that right now I need to accomplish things a little bit at a time. Don't feel bad if this is your reality too. It's okay—really.

Jump in. Get started. Tackle the big rocks. Even if you're busy, you will get there. (And maybe later you will get to Hawaii too!)

In this home, we chose to install hickory flooring throughout. The rustic two-toned wood transformed our space and provided visual connection between the rooms.

3

How Do I Start from Scratch?

I'm getting ready to move into a new home, and I'm trying to figure out which big piece—the paint color, the furniture, the floors, the cabinets, the curtains—I should start with. Inspiration is great for tying it all together, but I'm not sure how to begin when starting from scratch.

Samantha M.

KariAnne says...

A new home is a brand-new canvas for trying out anything you like—that paint color you've been dreaming of, the decorating style you've been trying to decide on, the flooring and the rugs you've always imagined. But before you shift your focus to *just one thing*, give yourself permission to make this home uniquely your own. Inspiration is everywhere. You can find it in decorating magazines and blogs and Pinterest boards and home décor shops—but start slowly. You don't have to make it happen all at once. A home wasn't decorated in a day.

1 **Start the process with something you're excited about.** Is there a certain color combination you've always wanted to try? A space—like a large entryway or a multipurpose room or a master bathroom—you've never had before? A room with a gorgeous view you just can't wait to style? This gives you a great idea of where to start. Begin where you're inspired and allow that inspiration to carry you into the other rooms of the house.

2 **How you decorate should be all about *you*.** If you want to turn a formal dining room into an art studio, go for it. If pink and orange are your thing, paint a room those colors. If you think a barn door makes the perfect coffee table, own it. Your house needs to be a reflection of you and who you are. Decorate with your heart and your home will follow.

3 **If you like bright colors but the magazines all say that neutrals are in, please don't listen.** This new space is your clean slate for decorating and designing in a way that makes you smile. If you are all about vivid hues and everyone is telling you to decorate with neutrals, hang the brightest colors you can from every corner of your house.

4 **Are you more of a minimalist?** Imagine an all-white room with a pink chair and a black table with a single lemon in the bowl as a centerpiece. If this image appeals to you, own it. Reduce clutter. Take the first step in creating a simple palette. Let that spill over into the rooms in your home, and then slowly add just a few statement pieces and pops of color as necessary.

5   **Pace yourself.** Learn to wait. I get it. I understand. I'm always running the decorating race so fast I get out of breath. Truth? If you haven't found just the right sofa or the perfect style of curtains, there's no hurry. Sitting on the floor never hurt anyone. Hanging up your curtains from your old home doesn't mean you have to display them forever. Great pieces will find you if you take your time.

6   **It's tempting to take care of big things first.** Large projects, such as painting a room, installing flooring, and hanging kitchen cabinets, make a mess and take time, so if you're absolutely sure what you want and it's in the budget, go ahead and begin. It's nice to get flooring and cabinet projects out of the way. If you're certain of your paint palette, start by using paint to transform your walls. But if you're still figuring out your style, press pause. Take a moment to make sure it's the look you want. Take it from my school of hard decorating knocks. I've painted a room five times to get the color right. I could have saved myself a few coats of paint if I had taken my time.

While neutrals dominate my décor, I love unexpected pops of colors. This vibrant navy background highlights a collection of whiteware and transforms the collection into a statement piece for the room.

Everything Needs Updating—Help!

My entire home needs updating. I'm overwhelmed with how much work needs to be done. How—and where—do I even start?

Barb S.

Melissa says...

I've been there, more than once! It's easy to become paralyzed when you feel that everything in your home needs to be redone, but the best way to begin is to make yourself start somewhere. Decorating can be especially frustrating when you feel you have the wrong house for your taste. You'd love to have a brand-new home or an old house with character, but you're stuck with a '70s or '80s home with no appeal at all as far as you can tell. Are your updating attempts and your trendy additions even going to make any difference at all with such a bleak background? Absolutely!

During some seasons of life, we just need to make the best of what we have and find contentment as we go. Creativity and a willingness to think outside the box will be your best friends when you're dealing with a dated home.

Depending on what you have to work with, you may need to begin with the foundational elements and later tackle decorating and organizational needs. Although it's far from fun, put your initial focus on big projects, such as removing icky carpet, adding in new wood floors, and putting a fresh coat of paint on every wall in the house. You'll find that these changes add an instant update *and* give you inspiration and vision for what your home could become.

When my family bought a 1950s house, we actually loved many things about it. But there were many things we *didn't* like. Sure, we would have loved to buy a house that was already perfect for us, but when we took into account our budget and time constraints, this was our best choice. As we set out to update the dated parts of the home, we realized that paint was about the biggest, most affordable game changer. And not just paint on the walls but also paint on the cabinets and shelves and doors. Identify what your home's game changer might be.

Homes stuck in another era often have ugly wood cabinets that you're longing to replace. But that replacement comes at a significant cost. Don't fear painting the wood. Once you add a coat of light, bright paint and install some fun new hardware—knobs and hooks—the transformation is nothing short of shocking. Suddenly dated and dull has become fresh and lovely (and that can give you the opportunity to enjoy your home even if you are still planning or saving for a remodel someday).

Updating a dated home can take a lot of time, and that's why I like to have at least one room in my home done before I do more extensive work around the house.

Depending on your needs, choose a bedroom or an office or someplace where you can rest and regroup when the constant stream of projects starts to overwhelm you. Finishing that one room can also motivate you and set plans in motion for the rest of your home. Eventually, you won't feel stuck in one era anymore.

In our 1950s home my husband and I started by painting our bedroom. We didn't know what direction we would go with the style of our home or overall color palette, but we needed one place where we could feel cozy and comfortable.

A coat of paint provided us a quiet retreat during the first few years, so it was worth it (even if it wasn't a color I was able to commit to forever).

After our kitchen was remodeled, we concluded the original color we chose for the bedroom was no longer right for us or the look we had adopted for our home.

While I agonized over repainting a "finished" room when other spaces were not yet touched, that paint had served us well for nearly three years.

A fresh coat of paint was relatively minor as far as projects went, but it was significant to how I felt about my home. It was the room we spent the most amount of time in! So don't let the possibility that you might not like a paint color choice years later stop you from loving your room right now.

One word about color: There are no "out" colors. It's all in how you present them that makes the difference. In the right doses, in the right places, all colors are still "in." So don't worry if you can't replace the bathroom tile or the kitchen flooring right away. Work with it and have some fun. Add an up-to-date wall color that mixes well with the features you don't love. Find some fun pillows and throws and towels that attract attention and detract from what isn't working for you.

As you take big or small steps toward changes, give yourself and your home grace. You might even find that some of those funky features are actually quite charming after all!

A fresh coat of paint in one room can give you a calm space to retreat to, even if the rest of the house is unfinished or still in process. The vision for our home evolved as other rooms were completed, so we later returned to this space to give it a new look.

How Do I Update Without Downsizing What I Love?

How can I improve my home's style without losing the things I love most about it?

Nancy S.

Melissa says...

You don't have to change everything at once. You can make changes little by little in a manner that feels right to you. This way you don't change something you love about your home in a moment of makeover frenzy. It happens!

Give yourself a solid starting place.

1. **Take a look at your home with fresh eyes.** Plan a 30-minute session to walk in your front door as though you were a guest. With your camera or your home journal in hand, walk around the house. Spend five minutes in each room. How does it make you feel? What *do* you love and like about your home? What one or two things drive you nuts, and the minute you look at them, you know they are not your style. Take notes or capture images of the aspects you don't like. Don't overanalyze. Five minutes in each room, tops. Those first impressions can tell you so much.

2. **Reflect on what you love most.** What gives you joy and adds a sense of story, history, or personality? If you have great pieces in your home, you should definitely keep them and use them. You might even find you love your traditional pieces even more than you thought you did once you embrace how really interesting a mix-and-match style can be!

3. **Take time to focus on less-loved features.** Decide what could be updated. Quality pieces are easy to update and refresh by adding pretty linens, a colorful throw rug, a modern mirror, some trendy lamps, plants in creative containers, or another decorating touch. And decide what should be removed from the premises, never to return again (heh, heh).

4. **Notice what catches your eye.** If you've been admiring some styles you've seen in magazines, blogs, or home décor stores, determine what two or three features are consistent in the images that grab your attention. You might be surprised how simply that desired style can be modeled in your home. Is the style you want primarily about tones, textures, backdrops, furniture, or accessories?

5. **Consider how those style features can be added to your home's look.** Do you need some color, more open space, a focal point, a unifying element in a room or area of the house, a furniture refresh of some kind, window treatments, a rug that centers a room? Is shifting toward a new style as easy as rearranging your furniture? You might be surprised!

6 Keep making adjustments, rearrange, and do periodic walk-throughs with fresh eyes. I've always loved just puttering around the house, trying things in new places, refreshing or styling small shelves, tables, or mantels, hanging things up on the wall, or adding to and displaying special mementos and collections. My favorite collections are ones that are of classic elements such as original art, pottery, and other timeless pieces. I love adding to a collection over time. It's a fun hobby, and it's a good way to decorate if you're not a big risk-taker.

Well-chosen and well-loved collections become a part of your style.

Always keep in mind that you want to preserve what you already love and care about. Remodeling can be rewarding, but there's something nice about taking your time and simply adding a few personal touches here and there. This way you have a style that can evolve *and* reflect your personality every step of the way.

A home should reflect your family's story. Even if you remodel your home from top to bottom, you'll feel most at home if you find ways to incorporate at least a few elements that connect you to special memories. These dinner bells in our kitchen belonged to my mom. Hanging them on the wall in our remodeled kitchen brought a welcome sense of nostalgia.

6

What's My First To-Do for a Redo?

I'm getting ready to completely redo one of the rooms in my house.
What is the first thing I should do to start the process?

Michele R.

KariAnne says...

Before-and-after-ing a room is so much fun—all the planning and the dreaming and the hoping and the imagining. But when it comes time to actually decorating the space, you find yourself stuck. Suddenly the whole process seems paralyzing. What should you do first? If you're having trouble starting your room renovation, here are three simple things to consider:

1. **Start with an actual plan.** You have a pile of accessories you've picked up and a file folder full of inspiration photos, but the cutest towels in the world won't help when your sink doesn't work or your bathtub is sitting in the middle of the garage. I once had an entire bathroom renovation planned with some of the cutest stuff on the planet—like a farmhouse sink, numbered baskets, and a reclaimed wood mirror—all ready to go. My design was on fleek, but I realized I was missing a few things. Like the shower. And the tub. And how a few of the walls should come tumbling down. That's when I realized the importance of a plan.

2. **You and your plan's best friend is a budget.** Truly. Because without a budget, you don't really have a viable plan. A budget isn't pretty or fun or inspiring, but it's practical and absolutely necessary. For

my before and after bathroom renovation, I was taking space from the master bedroom closet and another bathroom in the back, knocking down walls, picking out tile, and adding a shower, a bathtub, and a closet for towels and two sinks. With some planning, I put together a budget that worked. I figured out ways to cut costs in certain areas and go all affordable on items that weren't as big a priority to me. With the plan, I still had room in the budget to splurge on the must-haves and the things I really wanted.

3   **Make a list—and then keep adding to it.** It's like taking a trip to the grocery store. You think you've written down everything you need on your grocery list, but somewhere along the way you realize you're almost out of eggs. Then you remember you need Parmesan cheese for that pasta dinner and that your toilet paper supply is getting kind of low.

The same thing happens when you decide to redo a room. You sit down and make a list of everything you think you need, but then you think of one more item. And another. And then another. A list serves a dual purpose of helping you sort through the things you really need—like the eggs and cheese and toilet paper of the room—and it can also help you rule out extra items you think you want but might break your budget. You don't have to be too rigid with your list. It's important to leave room for inspiration. But a list can be just the tool you need to kick-start the process of a room remodel.

7

How Do I Set Project Priorities?

How do I prioritize projects around the house—both big and small? Is there a method to keeping the overload of plans and thoughts in order?

Angelika R.

Melissa says...

The best plan for getting started when you don't know where to start? Begin with something that really bugs you and move on from there. It's okay to go back and reprioritize. In our home we painted our dated stone fireplace so that we could enjoy our living room without the immediate expense of a more extensive project. The paint allowed us to move on to other significant projects and gave us time to think about what we really wanted to do in our living room. By this point you will have crossed something—or several somethings—off your wish list, and that always makes planning the next projects more manageable. And you can start off with a sense of accomplishment. Nothing is more motivating than seeing one area of your home transformed into a space you love to spend time in.

Even with a to-do list a mile long, there's always a way to prioritize your projects. When you're overwhelmed and don't know where to start or what to do next, a list or two (or three or four!) can be your best friend. Big-picture plans show the overall work that needs to be done, while daily task lists keep you focused on your goals for each day in priority order and help you focus on completing each task one by one until it's done. It helps me to use a large notepad or a daily calendar so I don't waste time searching for paper scraps or writing little notes in multiple locations.

When confronted with possible projects, be careful with your answers. It's impossible to say yes to every thought, idea, or request that comes your way. Give yourself time to weigh your decision. Remember, you can't do it all—in terms of both time and money! Choose what's most important to you and your family and let go of the rest.

Take a look at your life as a whole. I've been in situations where I know I can't spend a lot of time working on my home, but I've also been in seasons where I realized I was ready to focus my attention on my house—sometimes for a short period of time, sometimes for a more extended period—and cut down on travel and outside activities so I could really make some headway on big projects. Seasons come and go, but it's important to recognize and capitalize on the time you have available to finally dig in and get to work. Far from a frivolous pursuit, working on your home is a gift you can give yourself and your family. If you want your home to be a retreat from the world, caring for it and shaping it to your liking is an important priority that will make a big difference in your life and the lives of your family members.

When you invest your efforts in initially planning and prioritizing, you'll save time in the long run. You'll know what projects are next on your to-do list, and you'll feel more in control. You'll no longer feel there are SO MANY projects and rooms to do because you have clear objectives. You may still have a ton to do, but you can feel confident diving in and getting the ball rolling.

Remember, a home is never finished (which is part of the fun!), and you have permission to make mistakes and course corrections along the way.

AFTER

BEFORE

8

How Do I Create a Vision?

What are your top decorating tips for someone who doesn't naturally have a creative eye? How can I create a vision and add in the details to achieve a look I want?

Tylynn S.

Melissa says...

I love this quote from Coco Chanel: "Beauty begins the moment you decide to be yourself." You might think you don't have a creative eye, but I bet you know what you like and what you don't like. Trust your preferences as your guiding principle, and beauty will begin in your home.

When I'm stuck, I search for a look that appeals to me. You can start with a magazine, a home décor book, or favorite Instagram or Pinterest sources. When something catches your eye, save the image and keep gathering visuals. Next, lay out all the images so you can study each one and observe the collection as a whole. Certain commonalities and styles will likely emerge. You might discover you're drawn to bright hues or muted neutrals. Or that you favor eclectic designs or wood floors.

If the images don't represent the space, budget, or limitations you're dealing with, don't despair! It's time to establish your style for the space you *actually* live in. The great news? The best rooms evolve. To stay true over time to what you love, create a design board. Here are some tips on how to make one:

- Gather inspiration elements: mementos; patterns from scrapbook paper, fabric, and paint swatches; fonts; photos of furniture pieces; flowers; doodles; and dream lists.

- Arrange and secure the items to a bulletin board. The process of grouping and rearranging the colors, textures, patterns, and ideas will shape a vision.

- Hang the board where it will motivate you. Keep brainstorming and adding or removing items to bring your style to life.

- Take a photo each time you update the board for easy reference when shopping or gathering more elements.

Now that you're creating a vision, here are some easy ideas for adding personalized beauty:

1 **Find your jumping-off point.** Choose the key item that will be the most colorful or boldest piece in the room. Perhaps it will be a fabric for a pillow, a favorite piece of art, or a statement rug. If you're wary of commitment, choose a smaller accessory. Your key item can now direct your other decisions, such as what colors, patterns, and textures complement the design.

2 **Invest in something special.** Just one special piece can elevate the look of an entire room full of more humble pieces. Watch for deals on higher-end items and quality antiques at secondhand stores. A well-built sofa, a great cabinet, or a solid dining table create a foundation for a long-lasting beautiful style.

3 **Delight *your eyes and heart*.** What makes you happy? Look to your key piece, the jumping-off point, to inspire everything in your space. Confidently bring in elements you love and pair combinations of patterns and colors. You can even include a big "wow" piece for drama. Get rid of the rules and add in the joy.

4 **Add softness and curves.** Rooms with too many hard, square, and angular pieces are often less inviting than those with curves and interesting shapes. Try wingback chairs; a round coffee table, ottoman, or pouf; or a curvy lamp.

5 **Edit to let statements pop.** If too much is going on visually in a room, your style will be lost. Pick one or two statement pieces to take center stage (bolder fabrics or colors that pop, for instance), and edit out or tone down the rest. Best tip: Definitely edit out the clutter.

6 **Tell a story.** Express your story with the art, furniture, and accessories you add over time. Bring in history to your space with an older piece or ones with sentimental value.

Decorating a home is a process of discovering what you love and embracing what inspires you in whatever season you are in.

How Can I Realize My Vision?

What can I do when I have a vision for something I'd like to have, but I can't seem to locate it anywhere? From individual pieces to entire concepts, how can I make my decorating dreams a reality?

Liz M.

KariAnne says...

The challenge of inspiration mixed with perfection can be overwhelming. Sometimes we simply grab hold of an idea, and can't let it go. For example, we can't find the perfect paint shade. Or the just-right rug. Or the drawer pulls we *think* we once saw in Anthropologie. The stuff of our dreams simply doesn't exist—or if it does, it's way too expensive. But we keep looking for what we think we want, and when we can't find it…we do nothing.

This is the story of my decorating life.

Truth?

At some point, we have to let go of perfection and rethink our vision. When we refocus, sometimes a solution shows up in unexpected places. I once found a giant window on the side of the road. I knew it (and its 40 panes) had to be a calendar. I removed the glass, painted a piece of plywood with chalkboard paint, and attached it to the back. That window wasn't exactly what I was looking for, but it filled the big, blank wall in my living room with a unique piece of artwork.

The bedrooms and bathrooms in my home are full of items I found by thinking outside the box. I've created no-sew curtains out of drop cloths and layered patterned rugs over seagrass rugs to stretch my budget. I buy milk glass whenever I find it at thrift stores and yard sales, and I'm always on the hunt for unique pieces at second-hand stores—such as claw foot tubs and vintage sinks.

Here's what I want you to know: You can create a design vision that's uniquely you. Once you open yourself up to the possibilities, you start seeing options for your home everywhere. Does your design heart beat for hot pink and flamingos? Look and ye shall find. Are pale aqua and lace and chippy frames and cups that don't match calling your name? You will find those along your decorating journey. If your vision is gold and maroon and sparkly disco balls—well, that might take more time and ingenuity, but you never know when or where something might turn up.

Instead of focusing on one specific item, focus on a feeling, a vision, a look—and you'll know it when you see it. Then start looking for it in unexpected places—in the clearance aisles of a big-box store or on the shelves of the thrift shop or even in the forgotten boxes in your attic. Create your own look for your space, and your decorating dreams will become a reality. And then? Your rooms and countertops and cabinets and empty walls will be filled with the most important decorating accessory of all: your heart.

What Turns Great Deals into Great Designs?

My decorating budget isn't large, but I really love to hunt for fun items.
What are your best tips for using thrift shops and yard sales as your home design source?

Elizabeth E.

KariAnne says...

There are days when I'm driving down the road with super cute hair and red lipstick and sparkly flip-flops singing along with Taylor Swift on the radio, and then out of the corner of my eye I'll see the one thing that makes my heart beat faster: a multifamily yard sale sign. If you've ever turned in at a yard sale sign with hope springing eternal, come sit by me. Here are some of my favorite treasure-hunting tips:

1. **Be prepared.** Pack a little shopping kit to keep in your car. Mine includes a measuring tape, plastic bags for wrapping up delicate items, a screwdriver for taking things apart, and hand sanitizer (no explanation needed).

2. **Disregard color.** I can't count the number of times I've found the shape, size, or texture of the perfect piece, only to pass it by because the color threw me off. Color can be changed; however, the bones of an incredible piece cannot. Train yourself to look beyond the color to the actual piece you're buying.

3. **Imagine groupings and collections.** If you find a whole bunch of something you like, all of those somethings could look amazing grouped together. One time I found an entire basket of old letterpress stamps for almost nothing. One letterpress stamp? A little lame. A zillion of them stacked in a wooden container and hung on a wall? Amazing.

4. **In a thrift shop, grab a cart.** For some reason I always have better luck when I grab a cart at the entrance. I have no idea why, but I've found when you have a cart it manages to fill itself up.

5. **Always ask about the price.** Does the price seem too steep? Most of the time stores (and especially yard sales) price things a little higher just in case you ask. And the money you end up saving? Put it in your pocket. You might need it for the milk glass at your next stop.

Some of my very favorite things I use to decorate my home with came from a yard with a sale.

- **The dining room.** I have a $10 table that started out gray. I painted it white, and then I painted it charcoal. All of my white dishes? Every one of them came from a thrift store for less than a dollar. Bookcases *and* books

and the wood box I set on the bookcase to display my seasonal decorations? All thrifted.

- **The front entry.** Galvanized anything and everything. Creative, vintage, and unique signs.

- **The living room.** A dining table turned coffee table. A barn door that makes the perfect wall art and a stunning chandelier.

- **The family room.** Basically everything on my bookcases. Also, I found old keys I attached to pieces of molding to make an art display. The light fixtures in this room came from a yard sale too.

- **The laundry room.** Baskets, baskets, and more baskets. Also a five-dollar armoire (refinished and brought back to life).

- **The bedroom.** A two-dollar table, adorable decorative dishes, and the sign I display over the fireplace all came from thrift stores. Someone else saw something to discard, and I saw a treasure.

What Turns My House into a Home?

Where do I start to make a house feel like a home? I want to add my own personal touches, but I'm afraid the pictures or window coverings or paint colors will be all wrong.

Delora W.

Melissa says...

Don't worry about making a mistake! Most decorating decisions are not fatal (gratefully), and missteps can often be redirected or rescued. In fact, "mistakes" might even make your home more charming (I call these "happy accidents"). Here are some ideas to get you started:

- **When you add what you love, your house will feel like your _home_.** And those personal touches will very likely complement one another and provide a far more cohesive look than you'd have imagined. Every unique layer and personal touch will say, "This is me. This is my family. These are the things that make us happy. This is a place where people live and love and laugh." Let your choices work for you.

- **Add personal style and beloved pieces over time.** Give your home an interesting story to tell! Don't buy all your special touches in one or two shopping trips. We're most tempted to do this when we want a room "finished" for an event or a holiday, or when we want to play it safe by purchasing similar items from the same store, maker, or season. Rest in knowing that the perfect piece or combination of elements might take years to find. The

hunt is so much fun! And don't be surprised if a perfect piece or two finds _you_.

- **Enjoy the chance to wander through your rooms,** trying out different accessories in different places, moving and reshuffling pictures, and swapping out pillows and drapes. I'm constantly rearranging little displays and vignettes and moving collections around on the shelves until they feel just right to me. Oh, and one word when it comes to collections: Collecting things doesn't really set the tone in a home. But collecting things that have _meaning_ or that light up a corner of your home can definitely bring joy and a homey touch.

- **Give items something in common.** If a painting is of a different style or era than the curtains hanging near it, try a new location where it works better, or consider changing the frame so that it unifies the two décor features in some way. If you have three eclectic pieces of furniture, draw them together with similar trim treatments such as hardware styles or materials, create a comprehensive feel just by arranging these pieces in a cluster, or add a similarly colored accent item on each piece, such as a pillow, a vase, or a stack of books. In all these instances, your eye and mind will connect these items.

- **When it comes to the personal touches, don't make your to-do list too long.** But don't skimp on the details either. I'm drawn to tiny, charming details of life. In fact, even as I crave the simplicity of less stuff, I still thrive on the details. Those are what say "home" to me. Things such as flowers carefully arranged in a pitcher. A charming street sign. Sweet handwritten labels. Favorite plates and mugs stacked on the shelves. If it makes you smile and brings you joy, it's right for your home.

- **Enlist help!** If you feel paralyzed or indecisive on a home décor commitment (such as a new sofa or window coverings or paint colors), don't hesitate to ask the opinion of someone you trust. A second pair of eyes might give you more confidence to take the plunge or help you come to a better decision. Some designers or home décor bloggers online offer "e-design" packages that could help shape your vision or make decisions on key elements in a space. Retail stores sometimes have designers on staff who can offer helpful advice as you weigh your options.

Living in the Pacific Northwest, I'm inspired by the forest and the sea. I adore maps, compasses, ships, and other nautical or coastal elements. You can see that inspiration throughout my home.

Style & Trends

You've taken the plunge, maybe even completed—or at least started—a big project or two, and perhaps even purchased a few key pieces for your home. Now it's time to figure out your style. You want your home to look updated and current, but maybe the house itself is from another era. Can you really turn your ranch-style rambler into a beach cottage paradise? And that eclectic, vintage-y look you like...well, is it more trendy or tag sale?

It's easy to panic when you're assessing style and trends. No worries. Victory can be yours. You can blend your design plan and your budget, creating a home you love. With a few basic design principles, you'll have the confidence and the freedom to express your personality with a minimum of stress and second-guessing. *And then?* Just follow your heart. You've got this!

What *Is* My Style?

I'm attempting to hone in on my personal decorating style. I know the types of lamps, furniture, paint colors, and artwork I'm drawn to, but how can I identify my own style?

Kim G.

Melissa says...

I know how it feels to spend hours on end leafing through my favorite home and garden magazines or scrolling through Instagram looking for rooms that resonate. But rather than looking for a particular style to define my own look, I hunt for inspiration from a variety of homes and styles that speak to me. I call it the "observation game," and I've gone through it in each of the six homes I've called my own. It can be so helpful for discovering what you love. Sometimes, though, you can spend so much time on the paging and the poring and the pondering that you lose track of your own decorating style. If you're confused as to your personal style, or you find yourself stuck in the decorating process and unable to make choices or changes, it's time to put into practice my three favorite tips for identifying your personal decorating style:

1 **Brainstorm "inspiration words" to hone in on the style and mood of your home.** Think about places you love (or would like to one day visit); the style of your home's architecture; the landscape or terrain around your home; and inspiration from favorite books, flowers, hobbies, etc. You can even make a list of inspiration words to paint a picture in your mind of what you envision your home looking like someday.

2 **Make a list of treasures you'd like to collect or find over time.** Using your inspiration words, you can zero in on appropriate ideas to focus on as you move forward with your decorating. If the treasure matches one of the inspiration words, it's probably a good fit for your home. However, if it's a stretch to put it in any category, you might want to pass—no matter how great a deal it is. If your home currently feels cluttered with treasures and trinkets, you can use your list of inspiration words to weed out unwanted items. Does the item match your inspiration? If not, out it goes! Sometimes all an area needs is a little extra space to make it feel updated again.

3 **Find photos in magazines and images online that convey the *feeling* you want in your home.** You're not looking at the actual items—that sofa, this set of pots and pans, that light fixture. You don't need someone else's exact things, but you do want a similar environment and look. Find rooms that have something in common with your own rooms, such as the size and style of windows, similar room layouts, comparable architectural elements, or a home of approximately the same era.

This corner brought together a mood I love. Words that inspired me were "organic," "collected," and "coastal."

And don't worry about price. Recreating a look on a budget is fun—and can become addictive! It can become quite the game to get the look you want for less. Searching out dupes for everything from hand-painted mugs to holiday decorations is a great way to get the same feeling for less money.

Once you put all three steps together—the inspiration words, the list of treasures, and the photos that convey feeling—you're well on your way to understanding your own personal decorating style. And don't worry if it doesn't fit under a specific label like "farmhouse" or "beachy" or "modern." It's perfectly fine to mix and match elements as long as they all help contribute to creating the look you love.

How Do I Single Out My Style?

I love so many different decorating styles—I want to try them all! How can I decide on a consistent look for my home without making it seem as if I'm trying every style in the book? And how can I settle on just one style?

Corne H.

KariAnne says...

That's a great question. I officially have style ADD. I love them all. Beachy. Boho. French country. Modern. Classic. Shabby chic. Minimalist. So many décor styles, so little time. Sometimes they work when mixed together. And sometimes...not so much. My favorite style is farmhouse. I've loved galvanized metal and fruit-picker bushel baskets and white platters since way back before farmhouse was even a thing. To me, farmhouse says home. And kicking off your shoes. And sweet tea. And chalkboards and measuring cups and burlap curtains and mismatched chairs. That's the style I love.

To help define your style, start by making a list of the things you love. Look for the common denominator among the items on the list. Don't worry if you have items from different styles. Don't worry if you don't have one clear style. Your combination of different styles is your own.

Sometimes the problem might not actually be that you can't settle on just one style. It might be that you have *too much stuff* and that overwhelms everything else. I know. I get it. I understand. I've crossed the "clutter line" more times than I can count.

One fall I decided I was all about adding pumpkins *everywhere* in my fall décor. Seriously? Did every shelf of my home really need a pumpkin and a few friends? My kitchen looked as if all the milk glass went to a pumpkin convention and brought home a date.

Then there was the year I went all overzealous on my fall centerpiece. I started with a barn door. Then I layered in pumpkins and acorns and textured spheres. Then... *because that wasn't enough*...I added some white crinkle to round out the entire display and added a few vegetable friends in the background.

I've crossed the Christmas clutter line too. I decorated a mantel with white sprigs and birds and burlap bows and twigs from my yard and a few more finishing touches to try to make it perfect. It stopped saying farmhouse five twigs ago and started saying hot mess instead.

Do you see? Sometimes the problem isn't defining your style. Sometimes the problem is doing *too much* with that style. When that happens, stand back and observe, take a few things away, and allow the room to calm down. Sometimes you just need to stop and pause and tell yourself you don't need anything else. Your look is perfect just the way it is, and it's so much more than a label. Press pause on the clutter, and let your rooms breathe in your own style—a style that's just right for you and your home.

14

Help Me Sing, "I Did It My Way!"

I don't want my home to look Pinterest perfect or as though I copied it out of my favorite magazine. I like to do my own thing! Does every decorating decision have to follow a certain rule?

Laurie T.

Melissa says...

First of all, take a deep breath and repeat after me: *My home doesn't have to be perfect. I can create a home I love, and I don't have to follow the rules.* Say it a few more times to give you the confidence to do what *you* love. Now you can do your own thing and not worry about the "right" pieces or colors or design rules, I'll give you a few of my own guidelines. (Guidelines are take-it-or-leave-it bits of advice and are never to be confused with rigid rules! I'm a believer in becoming aware of decorating trends and rules so I can break them on purpose!)

1 **Add a splash of black.** If you feel that a room needs a little something, try a touch of black for contrast. If black is not one of your favorite colors, a bit of dark navy, gray, or green can provide the same visual punch in a lighter palette. Paint a door, a frame, or a dresser, or bring in a fabric pattern to make a striking statement.

2 **See straight.** Keep the pictures you hang at eye level (unless you plan to cover a large expanse of wall from top to bottom).

3 **Be inspired.** Choose one inspiration piece— perhaps a rug or a pillow—and build your color scheme and design around it.

4 **Paint last.** Instead of beginning with the paint color, end with it! That way you can make sure it goes with everything else in the room.

5 **Arrange for cozy.** If you have a large room, pull some furniture closer in and away from the walls to create a cozy feel.

6 **Go bold.** Select one statement piece for every room, even if it feels out of your comfort zone (but make sure it's something you love).

7 **Complement—don't copy.** Resist the temptation to match everything in a room. It doesn't have to match. It just has to *go*.

8 **Take time.** Collect what you love over time so your style will always be fresh and unique.

If you bring home a strikingly patterned item you've fallen in love with, like my curtains, let it inspire the entire room. Select a bold but pleasing wall color from the pattern. A deep color enveloping the space will let the pattern be a focal point and make your room feel unique and personal.

9 **Build on classics.** Stick with a classic style on key pieces and enjoy trends on easily replaced items.

10 **Personalize spaces.** Choose something whimsical and unexpected to add personality to each room.

There's also no set rule for how many decorative accessories should be in a room. That depends on your own personal level of comfort, but here are some guidelines I follow:

- I designate several visual clutter-free surfaces and wall spaces in a room in order to focus my creative energy on a livelier focal point. As much as I love color, pattern, and items that inspire me, I can also become overwhelmed by too much stuff if my eyes have no place to rest.

- I focus on simple bold or larger statements that are more striking and less visually distracting than a surface filled with many little items. Here's where baskets and fun containers can come in handy to corral the visual clutter.

- I create a home that is filled with the things I love, feels alive with the right amount of color and pattern for my personal preference, and brings joy to my daily life.

With time, you'll build confidence in making decisions for your own home! It doesn't have to resemble anyone else's. Feel free to get inspired by the style of others and then experiment.

I love this chandelier. Just by making one small change and adding this fixture to my room, the room felt transformed. (Total aside: I love this chandelier so much, one of my readers actually made me earrings inspired by it.)

What Will Bring My House into This Decade?

Besides a new coat of paint, what are some other ways to update your home? My house looks as if it's permanently stuck in 1990 with gold faucets and lighting fixtures and dated tile. How can I refresh its look?

Carrie D.

KariAnne says...

It can be hard to live in a home that's stuck in another era. The more you want to change it, the more glaringly the features you are not a fan of stand out. You want to change everything—the ceilings and the outside trim and the light fixtures from 1947. Eventually you probably *will* change some of these things, but in the meantime, your job is to love the home that is yours. Truth? Sometimes that's easier said than done.

When I'm feeling as if my home is less than perfect, I treat it as if it *is* perfect. I fluff the pillows in the living room and tell them how beautiful they are. I straighten the curtains in the dining room and remind the dining room chairs they're amazing. I stack my pretty bowls and mugs in the dishwasher and whisper softly to my kitchen that it's my favorite room in the entire house. By no means is my home perfect, but when I remind it how beautiful it is, I can start believing it *is* actually perfect—perfect for me and my family.

We can spend years and years striving to have the perfect house and the perfect us, but all that perfection is so overrated. The sooner we can let go of perfection, the sooner we can move on to enjoying the home we have and finding contentment. Strive for simple changes that bring happiness. Do what you can with the budget you have and table the rest for later. Make it your mission to choose a gorgeous color palette for your walls. Transform your front porch with a glossy coat of paint on the front door, add new house numbers or an updated light fixture, or hang baskets filled with gorgeous seasonal blooms. Invest in some fluffy bath towels and new hooks for the walls to bring a spa-like feel to a tired bathroom. Eventually you may get to the new siding or the updated cabinetry or the more modern light fixtures, but don't just wait around for *eventually* or *someday*. Take small decorating steps, adding a little something right now to make a difference today.

We have all been told not to compare ourselves to other people, and the same goes for our homes. Your home can't help the year in which it was born, so give it a little grace and then work with it right where it is. Continue to hope and wish and plan and dream, but also embrace your home today—even if it is a little worn around the edges and clinging to a previous decade. Keep adding the things you love to your home, and you'll discover that you and your house are perfect just the way you are.

How Do I Choose Timeless over Trendy?

I want to make decorating decisions that are not too trendy and will still be timeless in the years to come. How can I accomplish this?

Teryl W.

Melissa says...

You're asking for a decorating style that doesn't become dated but can evolve effortlessly through the trends? Me too! It's impossible to determine how long beach house or boho will be in vogue, but there are a few easy secrets to making sure your house will stay up-to-date longer than your yearly planner.

Focus on establishing a great foundation to mix, match, and layer with the new things you find along life's journey. You'll want your couch, dining table, and bed, for example, to be able to stand the test of time as foundational elements. Invest in classic shapes, styles, and materials for key furnishings so you are able to build a look that can ebb and flow though the evolution of seasons and styles.

Select pieces you know you will love for years to come. Items that can work in more than one space are an excellent choice. That way, you can shuffle furniture around to give your home a whole new look without spending additional money. By applying this simple decorating principle, your style doesn't become dated so quickly *and* it's flexible and more affordable.

Look for ways to incorporate items that are unique and meaningful so your home tells your story and perhaps some family history. I like using what you have (such as an heirloom or a longtime family-favorite piece) with something new.

When it comes to incorporating smaller details, have fun with the style and personality of each item. You can refresh an entire room by simply switching out a few accessories, mixing up the throw pillows, or adding new seasonal patterns and textures.

Only buy something because you love it, and don't worry about which trend or theme it fits. Remember—trends are just that. *Trends.* They don't last long, so incorporate them in small doses if you want to. Above all, don't overthink what works together in a space. Have fun changing things up, moving items around, and making decorating decisions based on what makes your heart happy.

To get the most bang for my buck, I choose timeless neutral furniture in classic designs and shapes so they can work in a variety of rooms and homes. The accessories and pillows are easy to update with the seasons and as styles change.

How Do I Keep My Style Consistent?

How do you make your decorating style consistent from room to room? I want my home to have some unity, but I also want each room to have its own personality.

Katie W.

KariAnne says...

I get it. I understand. You and your home want the same thing—unity. But creating that can feel a little overwhelming when each room seems to have its own individual personality. In a way, it kind of makes sense because each room serves a different purpose. The kitchen isn't going to look like your back porch. Your dining room shouldn't resemble your home office. The rooms in your home aren't going to be perfectly matched with each other. *But here's the best part.*

That's okay.

Sometimes I imagine what my home will look like when it's all grown up. Right now my home is a work in progress. It's in kindergarten—learning how to walk in a straight line and raising its hand when it has a question and discovering that Cheerios are the sixth food group. My home is still experiencing growing pains. One day it will get there. One day it will be ready for college.

One day it will look like Lucy's house.

When I first saw my friend Lucy's home, I had visions of what my grown-up house would look like. Her house is full of stories. Each piece of art, each antique, each handmade stool, each mirror and picture and rug has a tale to tell. As Lucy and I walked through the rooms, she told me stories

full of vivid descriptions and history regarding each item in her home. In the middle of the laughter and stories that swirled around us, I discovered something incredible.

I hadn't fallen in love with Lucy's house because it was a perfectly matched masterpiece with a consistent decorating style that flowed seamlessly from room to room. It wasn't the piano keys on the wall that turned my head or the giant oversized dough bowl on her kitchen counter or her basement ceiling that would look right at home in a contemporary art museum that made my heart beat faster.

It was *how* she decorated, not *what* she'd used to decorate.

Lucy understood how to breathe life into a space and wrap her guests in welcome from the very first moment they stepped through the front door. Her decorating plan—that plan that worked to show consistency *and* personality throughout the entire home—was to surround herself with friends and family, collect what she loved, and let her heart do the decorating.

Why not apply that to my own home?

I *could* let myself be bothered by the scraggly Walmart Christmas tree without a skirt. Or the white pumpkins I'd inadvertently left out by Mary and Joseph and baby Jesus.

Or the dust on the bookshelf. Or the set of encyclopedias that the dog had chewed. *But why?* The reality is—that's me. I'm just a girl who wears cheetah print shoes with ripped jeans and big earrings. I like spray paint. And chips and dings and character and imperfections. I adore glitter and barn wood and milk glass and things from the clearance aisle I never even knew I needed. And my home? It's perfectly imperfect, and it works for me. But more importantly, I want to remind myself that no matter the steps on the journey, no matter how many decorating mountains are left to climb, no matter what grade my house is in…

It's *perfect* just the way it is.

If I could give you one piece of design advice, one favorite decorating tip for having unity and consistency in your style and personality in each and every room, it's what Lucy and her house taught me: *Decorate from your heart, and let the rest take care of itself.*

This transition from kitchen to entry to office showcases each room's personality. From farmhouse to traditional, the rooms flow seamlessly due to a similar color palette and carefully curated accessories and furniture.

Is My Dream of Two Themes Too Much?

I'm finding it difficult to decide on a theme for my home. I love both the farmhouse look and the beachy look. I'd like to incorporate elements of both into my rooms. How can I do this?

Haley G.

KariAnne says...

I love the farmhouse style. I can't help it. I love chippy old pieces and vintage finds and fresh flowers and things that need rescuing and shopping the side of the road. But I also love the beach look. Here are some fun tips for incorporating both farmhouse and beach into your home. Choose your favorites from these lists and blend the two styles effortlessly together.

FARMHOUSE

1   **Fresh flowers.** I cannot overstate this enough. A little milk glass makes a flower even prettier. One piece of milk glass is fun, but encourage it to take a trip to milk glass land and bring some relatives home.

2   **Painted furniture.** Adding a piece of painted furniture makes the whole space yours, especially if you are the one who painted it.

3   **Natural fiber rugs.** Seagrass is an inexpensive option to consider when selecting an area rug, and it's a material that holds up well in high-traffic areas.

4   **Neutral-colored curtains.** When you're going for the farmhouse look, don't overthink your curtains. I actually have some drop cloth curtains I pinned in place one day. I meant to go back and sew them, but why? The pins are working so well.

5   **Architectural details.** One of the easiest ways to add character to your home is with architectural detailing. For example, I had a too-small mantel I added crown molding to and painted white. Now it's the focal point of the room.

6   **Ticking stripes.** Introduce a little ticking into your life—preferably on a bolster pillow or a vintage bed—with a red-and-white quilt. And a really good book.

7   **Vintage.** Create an authentic farmhouse look with vintage finds. Layer in pieces such as ladders, windows, and even frames made from barn wood.

BEACH

1 **Painted floor.** Nothing says, "Welcome to my ocean" like a painted floor. You can paint it turquoise. Or red. Or pale blue. Maybe just one room or a runner in the hallway. But beach it up with paint.

2 **Vintage.** Mix a vintage sink with a vintage medicine cabinet with a vintage shelf. The result? Vintage perfection.

3 **Adirondack chairs.** I have four of these at the beach house. They are white and came from Walmart. But those ocean breezes make them look like high-end design.

4 **Screened-in porch.** I try to never invite bugs to my party.

5 **Planked walls.** Simple and serene. And easy— just plywood boards painted white. *Yes, please.*

6 **Wood.** Every beach house needs a little original wood. A vintage trunk. A wooden bench. An antique hutch. And driftwood, of course.

7 **Vintage letters.** Create your own out of pallet wood, or search for them at thrift shops and junk stores. Spell out a beach word for your wall.

8 **Souvenirs.** But not the kind you buy from a tourist stand. The kind you collect. Add a basket of shells. Collect a bowl of rocks. Paint an inspiring word or Scripture reference on a sand dollar. Add a little beach sand and some flowers to a mason jar. Create a sign or mirror or picture frame from driftwood. And then? Let the sunshine in.

Can I Create One Style Under One Roof?

I can't seem to get my home to flow like the homes I see in magazines and online. How do I make my whole house decorating style seem cohesive?

Lily G.

Melissa says...

When you love different styles, a home can go through some awkward phases, can't it? I've been there, where nothing seems to fit or flow. Trying to create a cohesive design throughout a home (or even in a room!) can feel tricky, particularly if you are working with a mix of pieces you've collected over time.

You might have pieces you still find beautiful from your English country phase and a couch you fell in love with when you decided to go mid-century. You might have collected a few items from the time you decided bright yellow was going to be your signature color or when owls were all the rage (and your entire family gave you owl figurines for Christmas). I get it.

When you look at inspiration on Instagram, you might wonder if the only options for a cohesive style are either to pare down to one look or simplified color palette or start over completely. Of course, those can definitely be options. Yet as put together as a home may look when everything matches perfectly, an acquired style can be unique and so much more interesting! Best of all, it tells a fun story of your journey.

The secret to making a variety of pieces or styles feel more harmonious and even intentional is a process I call connecting the style dots. In order to create a cohesive look, you simply need to establish some visual connectors throughout the room and your home. Similar to the process of creating flow in an open floor plan (as we'll talk about in question 47) you can begin to create more continuity with your style in five ways.

1 **Color continuity.** Simply repeating a color several times within a room or around your home creates a sense of continuity. The repetition of a color tells your eye that the design of the space (and everything in it) is intentional and holds together.

2 **Style statements.** Use key statement pieces to tie elements together. It can be as simple as using two or three pillows in the same pattern fabric on a sofa or adding one large patterned or natural fiber rug that can bring together various pieces of furniture.

3 **Architecture.** Architectural elements in your home can be repeated to bring greater continuity to the style. Repeat the same style of doors or hardware throughout. Add molding or repeat a style of woodwork in several rooms. Repeat metals in faucets or lighting.

Use a consistent or similar color palette for flooring throughout the house. Even if you can't do all of these things, start with what you can do. Your eye will pick up on any repetition.

4   Accessories. Two matching lamps can bring continuity to an eclectically furnished space. Several accessories in the same color scheme or shape can make the design feel more intentional and help draw your eye around the room.

5   Style. Even if you love a lot of styles you want to incorporate in a room, repeat at least one style (or even a shape of furniture) enough that it pulls everything else together (a matching set of chairs, for instance, can work well). To use farmhouse as an example, if you love farmhouse but want a mix of styles in your home, adding one farmhouse-style antique in several rooms can be enough to make the statement. You can also create style continuity with a repeated shape, such as having several straight-lined pieces around your home.

20

Can I Translate a Style into My Décor Language?

There's a look that I love, but I'm not sure if it goes with the style of my home.
How can I interpret a certain look while taking into consideration the type of home I live in
(e.g., beachy look in a contemporary home or modern look in a cottage-style home)?

Sandy C.

KariAnne says...

Repeat this important decorating rule after me: *I don't have to let anyone else tell me what to do.* Say it strong. Say it like you believe it. Say it with confidence. If you adore doilies, but all the decorating magazines and blogs proclaim that doilies are so 1990—doily up your house anyway. If you love pink with orange but your mother-in-law insists that those colors don't go together—cover your house in pink and orange anyway. And if you're dreaming of the farmhouse look, but your sleek, modern condo is trying to tell you otherwise—embrace the farmhouse style you love.

It's empowering to be a decorating rebel, isn't it? Even if the architectural details of your home don't scream coastal or contemporary or bohemian, bringing the unexpected to your interiors (and exteriors) adds a touch of whimsy. You may not be able to change your walls or windows, but you can layer in *patterns* to state your style. Keep these patterns in mind when you're choosing linens, furniture, window treatments, rugs, and even smaller accessories such as pillows and throws. Here are five favorite combinations to consider:

TRADITIONAL

Large-scale pattern: overall floral
Medium-scale pattern: 1" stripe
Small-scale pattern: tiny starburst
Solid: linen

WHIMSICAL

Large-scale pattern: abstract graphic
Medium-scale pattern: swirls
Small-scale pattern: tiny polka dots
Solid: velvet

BOLD

Large-scale pattern: large geometric print
Medium-scale pattern: graphic chevron
Small-scale pattern: mini stripe
Solid: metallic sheen

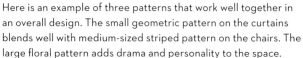

Here is an example of three patterns that work well together in an overall design. The small geometric pattern on the curtains blends well with medium-sized striped pattern on the chairs. The large floral pattern adds drama and personality to the space.

NEUTRAL

Large-scale pattern: faded oversized damask
Medium-scale pattern: geometric
Small-scale pattern: tiny stripe
Solid: woven texture

FARMHOUSE

Large-scale pattern: large polka dot
Medium-scale pattern: colorful floral
Small-scale pattern: gingham check
Solid: linen

Here an oversized damask gives us our large-scale pattern which coordinates well with the medium-scale buffalo check. Finished off with the small-scale ticking, these patterns work together to create pattern magic while also celebrating your style.

I cannot overstate this enough. If you like wood stumps or neon plastic tables or exit signs or 50 clocks on a wall, and no one else agrees with your design choices—design it anyway. Your house doesn't need to look as though it stepped straight out of a magazine. It just needs to look as though it stepped straight out of your heart. So decorate with confidence—and don't allow anyone to tell you what you *have* to do.

21

Will My Beach Style Cross a Line in the Sand?

I love the beachy, coastal vibe. How can I achieve this look without overdoing it—especially during the non-summer months?

Wendy C.

Melissa says...

I'm in love with coastal style. Not only do I adore the lifestyle it represents (which is the key to an authentic style), but I also love that you can interpret "coastal" in so many different ways. Whether you live on the East Coast or the West Coast, or have lived and traveled abroad to an entirely different coast, you have the freedom to interpret this style in the way that best fits *you*.

No two beachy rooms have to to look the same! Do watery, soft blues appeal to you? Make that your look. Are you wishing for a bolder style? Stick with the tried-and-true nautical red, white, and blue. Also assess whether you're more vintage, more modern, or more natural. See how many different ways there are to interpret this style?

Regardless of the direction you want to take your beach inspiration, here are some tips to make your home fit a coastal vibe:

- Decorate with some potted palm plants for a nod to island style.

- Fill a modern-style home with neutral whites and grays, and then add tasteful textures such as seagrass rugs, bamboo shades, or woven baskets for additional warmth and interest.

- Eliminate the heavy curtains and go with bare windows or breezy sheers and shutters.

- Think subtle style statements. Striped rugs or nautical lanterns add an authentic and classic coastal feeling to your home. A porthole mirror is seasonless and more attractive than tacky tourist accessories.

- Wainscoting or painted paneling provides a room with coastal cottage texture.

- Bring the ocean into your home with subtle hints of pale blue and green glass lighting and accessories.

- Frame elements from the sea in your main living spaces.

- If you want to make a bold statement, wallpaper bathrooms and small areas with playful paper of ocean creatures and marine life.

- Display coastal collections such as rocks and shells in glass jars. You can even add decorative labels that proclaim where you collected your treasures. You always have the option to put away these mementoes in the winter and bring them back out in the summer!

Bathrooms or powder rooms can be a simple space to bring in a little extra coastal flair. A bathroom is a smaller space with most of your big pieces (sink, tub, shower, and toilet) already in place. A bathroom makeover usually just involves a fresh coat of paint, an updated shower curtain, and some inexpensive, easy-to-change-out accessories. Try hanging your towels with a nautical-style rope or painting your vanity an oceany shade of blue.

Feeling ready to kick off your shoes and dig your toes in a sandy beach? Me too! Last I checked, there are quite a few coasts in this world and they are all different. That should give you plenty of permission to make some waves with your favorite retreat-by-the-sea style. No matter how you interpret your look, you can create an atmosphere evocative of cool breezes blowing off the water and the warm sand under your toes. And that *feeling* is the best part of coastal living, isn't it?

Should Leather and Lace Ever Marry? Speak Now.

Major decorating dilemma here. I like flowers and romantic touches throughout my home, but my husband prefers brown leather and deer heads! How can I properly mix such strong feminine and masculine preferences?

Cindy R.

KariAnne says...

I completely understand the challenge, so I'd suggest trying a decorating style that combines your different aesthetics in a unique way. You don't have to designate separate his and hers rooms in your home. Strive for a more neutral palette, adding in small and understated touches of the things each of you prefer. For example, introduce the floral prints you love with accent pillows rather than statement pieces, such as an accent chair. Choose florals and prints in darker colors to accent the masculine pieces.

Here are five specific ways to combine masculine and feminine décor:

1 **Nature.** Combine the earthy tones of masculine décor with greenery and potted plants and more feminine décor with vases of fresh flowers.

2 **Color.** Introduce elements of masculine décor with darker hues, such as navy and shades of orange, and then layer in more feminine colors in a space, such as white, gray, coastal blue, and taupe.

3 **Texture.** Juxtapose leather with softer, more feminine textures such as linen and woven fabrics.

4 **Accessories.** Let each person's personality shine through in a room. Introduce pieces that represent the design style of each individual. For example, more masculine accessories might be items such as maps, globes, leather-covered books, or antler sheds. Feminine accessories might include a floral pillow, a vintage sewing box, or a milk glass vase. Editing accessories is the key to making the overall design in the space work.

5 **Plan spaces.** If deer heads are a must, create a space just for them. Design a den with plaids and leather and vintage masculine décor. In equal opportunity decorating, create another space filled with more feminine décor and accessories.

Truth?

You want to create a home and spaces where everyone can feel that they have a place. Simply try to incorporate thoughtfulness and purpose when combining feminine and masculine design styles. Then harmony will reign.

Can I Connect My Eclectic Pieces?

I have a lot of really cool pieces I've collected (furniture, rugs, artwork, accessories), but I'm having a hard time tying them all together. Do you have any ideas on making an eclectic mix work?

Janine R.

Melissa says...

I'm your biggest cheerleader for decorating a home with collected pieces that have special meaning to you. Just because you have an eclectic mix of items doesn't mean you won't be able to have a style that makes sense. There's no real label for my style anymore, but I *like* that I can't pinpoint it or even describe it. It isn't fully cottage. Or fully traditional. Or modern. Or French or English or American. And that's just fine. That said, *too much* undefinable style can result in a mish-mash that doesn't feel pulled together. You can make your special, personal mix work by keeping a few pointers in mind.

1 Use color repetition to weave pieces together. When you repeat an element or a color in a room multiple times, it looks more cohesive and intentional. For example, if you have a red chair you love but feel it just doesn't go with anything else, consider adding a red lamp to the opposite side of the room and even artwork with a touch of red in it too. Once the color appears at least three times, you'll begin to feel that your room is more cohesive and the red is no longer the odd piece in the room.

2 Use a rug as a room unifier. A rug can tell your eye that everything on it belongs in the room. It can visually pull an entire collection of furniture together because it covers such a large amount of space. If your furniture has a lot of color, pattern, or personality, look for a natural rug (sisal, seagrass, or a rug in a solid or neutral) to be the unifier. If you have a lot of neutral or wood pieces, a patterned or colorful rug can make a style-setting statement.

3 Pair things up. When you collect great pieces over time, you've likely wound up with an interesting mix of furniture and accessories. How fun is that? But because your eye isn't sure which delight to enjoy first, you might feel as if your style is a little chaotic or as if your room doesn't hold together. Here's a trick that can make sense of it all. Pair up related items. If you have two chairs that happen to match or are of similar shape, style, scale, or fabric, place them side by side or immediately opposite each other. Create a statement with a pair of lamps on a console table. Pair up matching or eclectic candlesticks and line them up on the mantel. Make a collection out of random accessories that are in the same color family or material.

4 **Streamline.** If you have excessive things or too many unrelated pieces that just don't seem to work together, try streamlining and forming new combinations that inspire you. Move items around to other rooms to experiment. You might find that when certain pieces are placed in a new room, you are happier with the look or combination in both spaces.

I much prefer a gathered-over-time look to an I-ordered-it-all-from-the-same-collection style. Enjoy the freedom of not being able to pigeon-hole your style—to not feel confined by what is expected.

Can I Say Yes to Eclectic and No to Chaotic?

My favorite look is an eclectic look, but I'm worried that the elements I pull together will end up clashing. What are some ways to tie an eclectic look together?

Cecilia B.

KariAnne says...

The items you love all have something in common: the fact that you love them. At first glance the combination of objects might seem kind of random, but when you look at the group as a whole, you'll notice that there are some common colors, textures, or patterns.

Quick tip: You can always transform the items you love to make them fit the existing décor a little better. Spray paint and fabric are just waiting to be your best friends. In addition, one of my favorite ways to tie an eclectic look together is by creating a collection.

- **Anything can be a collection.** Truly. Just find something that makes you smile. I've collected teapots and frogs (the floral decorating kind) and baskets and blue-and-white plates and milk glass and license plates. Even certain colors and textures and materials can function as a collection of sorts, such as a collection of a certain color or type of glassware or dishes or linens.

- **Look around your house.** What do you have multiples of? What always catches your eye when you're out shopping or looking at someone else's home? You may have a collection—or a collection in the works—right under your nose and not even know it.

- **Once you've established your collection, begin to group the items together.** One item alone is simply an accessory. But a mantel filled with a dozen of the same item? It's a statement. I like to display collections on a tray (like a bunch of wooden blocks) or in a bowl (a few handfuls of Scrabble tiles). Group larger collections in baskets or crates. You can even create a wall display with your collection.

- **Think outside the box.** Sometimes it seems as if everyone is collecting the same thing. This has two challenges. First, if everyone wants it, the price goes up, and that makes it expensive to collect the item. Second, if everyone has it, it's trendy, which means at some point it's going to go out of style. That's where the unique and the eclectic work well. If you think outside the trends, your collection is always fresh and new—and usually more affordable as well.

- **If you're tired of looking at a collection, don't be afraid to let it go, wish it well, and show it the door.** Nothing personal. The collection may simply not be for you anymore. Donate it, give it away, or even repurpose it into other décor in your home.

How Do I Make Heirlooms Feel at Home?

I own some meaningful antiques I've inherited from my family. How can I use them in my home, especially when they don't seem to fit my existing decor?

Barbara I.

Melissa says...

Whether it is a vintage accessory or a well-crafted piece of furniture, I adore things of quality and age. And a family piece has an even stronger presence and beauty. If you love it, here are some ways to welcome an heirloom piece into your home:

1 Expand your style. These antiques are a gift because they allow you to create a look all your own. Don't force a piece into a trendy style; instead, allow your style to include that piece. For example, a vintage chest placed as a side table next to a contemporary settee offers a striking style contrast.

2 Embrace eclectic. If antique furniture you have from family or from rounds of shopping estate sales and flea markets are of varying types of wood and materials, you have a few options. Unify the random look with new hardware, upholstery, or paint. Or let like items shine together in a nook, a room, or an area of a room.

3 Welcome the warmth. If you have a room that seems to lack ambience and character—a room that seems a little too fresh-from-the-discount-home-store—these antiques will come to your rescue. Vintage items can really grab your senses. Think how solid wood, vintage textiles, oil paintings, delicate china cups, or cozy braided rugs invite guests to touch them and enjoy their beauty. They make your home more personal and more welcoming.

These items were created to last, and often their beauty becomes more pronounced with time. You can enjoy them for their attractiveness and craftsmanship, not for their trendiness. You and your family will appreciate how these pieces warm up a room.

4 Showcase and connect pieces. If a piece is quite different from anything else you own, let it be the focal point in a room. For example, if you inherit an oak roll top desk and your furniture is mostly white-washed wood, center that desk against a wall so that the warm tones draw the eye. It could have the same impact as a fireplace and mantel—soothing and centering. You can even place a whitewashed accessory on the desk to tie it to the rest of the look. Connect your pieces without forcing any of them to be something they aren't.

5 Celebrate the benefits of antiques. Trendy décor can be expensive when we strive to keep up with what's hot and what's not. Antiques last and will provide you with some consistent pieces that then allow you to play with trendy touches without breaking the bank.

6 Take a risk. It is worth it. Pull those antiques out of the closet or attic. Mix them with new items, and then mix them some more. Instead of being worried about what is right, proper, popular, or acceptable in the world of decorating, push the envelope on creativity. Arrange and rearrange. See what resonates with your soul. Look at time-loved objects in new ways and consider them in different rooms of your home.

To make your home a true reflection of who you really are, strive to have a unique collection of things other people couldn't possibly have because you found them in a thousand different places and moments in time. Items that already have a history of their own are even more special. It's fun to know a piece was around way back when and has its own unique story to tell—a story far more interesting than any discount home store accessory could ever dream up. The modern, the quirky, the reinvented, the antique, and the memorable can all happily coexist in your personality-filled rooms.

My grandparents brought this gorgeous chinoiserie chest home with them from Thailand. My dad remembers playing with it as a child, as he was quite fascinated with all the drawers and hidden compartments! Family heirlooms can hold a place of honor in your home, whether you feature them prominently in your design or use them as a functional piece in a less conspicuous corner.

Here's the family room after a Gilmore Girls marathon. Couch turned askew. Cushions tossed to the floor or squashed into submission. Popcorn bowl next to the fireplace. The tables hold glasses with orange juice still in them. This is the life!

Can a Kid-Friendly House Be Style Friendly?

I love decorating, and I also love my young children! I dream of having a cute, cozy, and creative home where my kids can play to their hearts' content but that also looks warm and welcoming and well designed. Is this an impossible dream, or is there a way to make it happen?

Amy N.

KariAnne says...

When my children were younger, it wasn't easy for me to decorate my home. I had four little people under the age of six. I'd add a pillow to the couch. They'd un-pillow it. I'd put blankets in a basket. They'd un-blanket it. I'd stack books with metal spheres on the coffee table. They'd un-book it. It always takes a little longer to decorate when you are decorating with friends.

Now that my kids are older, decorating looks a little different. Instead of taking away the décor, they add to it. My teenagers add plates of pizza crusts and water bottles and homework and almost empty bowls of Honey Nut Cheerios. They sprinkle the room with shoes and coats and basketballs and baseball bags and sweatshirts and stinky socks.

Me? I try to hold on to every stage. Every minute. Every stinky sock. It all goes by so quickly, and I want to enjoy it. I want my family to feel welcome in the home. So for now I try to balance everything—my kids' current needs and my own decorating dreams. Letting go of perfection helps. I try to embrace the here and now and know that happiness can be found amid the mess. Just in case you needed an example of a mess I blessed, let me give you a mental snapshot of some incriminating scenes in my own home. May my less-than-perfect life help you to celebrate your own piles, stashes, and kid-created "décor" moments.

First up, let's take a tour of my kitchen and wave to the dishes stacked in the sink. Say hello to the rolls of paper towels on the counter. Watch for the dirt on the floor that was tracked in after a spontaneous outdoor football game. Just in case you were missing the mixing bowl—it's in the living room holding the remains of the popcorn.

Moving right along, be sure to survey the living room. It is a hot mess. The flower arrangement? It used to be gorgeous, but it has seen better days, and now its petals are dropping like crazy all over the counter. Tiny people have spent the afternoon in here drawing and glittering and decorating and leaving a trail of scraps to the door. And, of course, a pile of stuff is on the floor. Nobody really remembers what's in it because it's been there so long.

Nothing like living the dream. Truth? I am—I'm decorating and mothering all at the same time. Often it feels as if I'm taking two steps forward and one step back. But the journey has a great view along the way. Look around your own home and see for yourself. There truly is beauty in the chaos.

What Can I Update Without a Budget Upset?

I'm ready for a change of style, but I can't justify added expenses. What is the best way to update and give a new feel to my home when the budget is tight?

Mindy H.

Melissa says...

It's frustrating to be limited by finances, especially when the decorating bug hits. And when I see an item I just *know* would be perfect, but my bank account doesn't agree? Absolute torture! Yet sticking to a budget is important and will result in a great reward for your décor options later. Making it your own doesn't require that you make the design perfect; rather, it's about creating a home that feels right for your family in the season you are in.

I'm a firm believer that updating your look oftentimes can be accomplished on a limited budget and with just a few simple changes. You might not know this little tidbit, but *The Inspired Room* didn't start out as a blog. It began as a redesign service! I loved going into women's homes to help them reimagine their style. Together we could give a room an entirely new look in one afternoon, often by using what they already had in a fresh way.

While I'd love to pop over to your home right now to help you do the same, here are four strategies you can use to give your space a budget-friendly new look! Perhaps enlist a spouse or friend to help and make the whole process more fun.

1 **Redesign in a day.** If you are longing for a significant change, take everything out of the room, repaint if you want to, and then add back in only what you still love or want to use. Before you return furniture to the space, a new rug could update your style and make the room feel entirely different. A seagrass rug can be affordable and works with many styles and upholstery items you might already have. Once the rug is in place, bring the furniture back in and create a cozy conversation area!

2 **Mini makeover in an afternoon.** Remove from the room only the things you *really* dislike. Definitely eliminate all the clutter and knickknacks. Once a room is decluttered, it may feel a bit bare, but live with it that way for a few days. You might find you like it as is, or a clean slate may spark a fresh vision for the next step in reimagining your style.

3   Quick and easy updates. Here are some things that can be changed easily and on a budget (even over time if necessary) to give any room a new style:

- refreshed window treatments

- stylish accent pillows

- a new throw or a scarf over the back of a chair

- new or refurbished lamps and/or lampshades

- one bold statement piece to replace several knick-knacks you have grown tired of

- new or repainted frames and new mats for photos

4   Shop your home. One thing you can do immediately—and costs no money at all—is "shop" your home. Wander through various rooms hunting for items in drawers or cupboards you can bring out and give new life to in a different setting. Switch up the furniture by using conventional pieces in unconventional ways to keep your home's look fun and fresh. Bring the dresser you had in your bedroom to the living room and the lamps that were in the living room to the bedroom. *Voil*à! Instant makeover.

Look around at what you have tucked in storage areas. You might find some paint in the garage you can use to give a wall or a piece of furniture a new hue. That fabric stash you've been collecting forever? Whip up some simple pillow covers or a seasonally appropriate tablecloth.

Once you challenge yourself to decorate with the items and materials you have on hand, creativity begins to awaken!

The Major Elements

The major design elements of each room are the pieces that really define your style and give your home the atmosphere you crave. But blending all of these elements can be tricky. Should you choose hardwood floors throughout the house or mix in a little carpet here and there? Where should you place your area rugs? How do you work around existing windows—or a lack of them—to make certain each room has sufficient lighting? And what are clever and unique ideas to decorate your walls?

The good news is that you have a lot of options, and you don't have to follow a bunch of rules. Your style is your own, and you don't have to limit yourself to one particular style when it comes to coordinating the various elements of a room. Use your creative vision and layer different elements you love—even if they don't match in a traditional sense— and you're one step closer to achieving a look you love and making your home uniquely *yours*.

What Are the Foundational Guidelines for Flooring?

How important is it to have the same color and type of flooring throughout your home? When should you replace carpet with hardwood flooring (like in a bedroom)?

Jody G.

Melissa says...

Flooring may not be the first thing we think of when it comes to decorating, but the type of flooring in a house plays such an important role in the overall design and feel of the home. It can also have quite an influence on decorating decisions and renovation plans we make. Whether you have to live with the flooring already in your home or you're able to start from scratch and select options that suit your home's style and your personal preferences, it's possible to turn your flooring into your greatest décor asset.

While consistent flooring throughout connecting rooms can make a home feel more spacious as your eye flows effortlessly from room to room, it's not always an affordable or even a preferable choice. Kitchens, bathrooms, and bedrooms are often spaces where it might make sense to change flooring for cost, comfort, style, or durability. Carpeting a bedroom, for instance, can be a very cozy choice! If you're building or remodeling, you might choose to have fun with creative flooring options.

If you have the budget and the time to put in all new wood flooring, yay! There's nothing quite like the look of hardwood floors to replace old, stained carpet and damaged flooring. There are so many beautiful types of wood floors: gorgeous varieties and grains of wood; endless options of stains, finishes, and flooring widths; and a multitude of patterns that can be laid to create beautiful custom patterns and designs. Strive for a look and finish that fits your family's lifestyle, budget, and the existing elements of your home.

If you want a quick, inexpensive solution to update existing carpet, you can layer an area rug right over it. I really love the look and texture of sisal and seagrass rugs. You can also use oriental rugs or any other type that makes you smile. Layering rugs over carpet might break some design rules, but that's fine if a new rug could make you happy enough to forget about the not-so-attractive carpet underneath!

Another way to get a flooring look you love? Paint the subfloors! If the carpet you have is just too horrible but new flooring isn't in your budget, this can be an economical option. It takes some effort, but sometimes life is too short to hang on to the ugly until someday. Rip out those carpets, clean the floors, paint them a solid color (making sure you sand and prime so the paint will stick), and pop a few rugs on top. Sometimes a temporary solution works so well that it becomes permanent!

Which Flooring Options Are Best?

My current floors are a mess, and I'm ready for all-new flooring,
but I have no idea what type to choose. What are the alternatives to carpet,
and which types of floorings work best in certain rooms?

Shelley G.

KariAnne says...

You may not get as excited about flooring as you do about paint or furniture or accessories, but flooring deserves a spot in your decorating heart. It's the unsung hero of the home improvement world and the design foundation of any space. It's often overlooked because, typically, it's one of the most expensive design elements in a room—and one of the hardest to change. You can move furniture in and out of various rooms. You can paint your walls five times in one year. You can change your curtains and your pillow covers and the pictures on your wall in a weekend. But the floor? It's a permanent resident. That's why it's so important to educate yourself on all your available flooring options.

Here's an outline of different types of flooring choices. When deciding on flooring, you want to keep in mind the cost, how easy each material will be to clean, and how much effort each will take to install. It's also important to take into consideration the purpose and style of the room, whether or not you typically wear shoes in your house, and who will be using the room most often.

HARDWOOD

Try one of the most popular and sustainable flooring options on the market today. Hardwood is durable, long-lasting, and sustainable, wood is a natural material that adds authenticity to your home. Wood floors are also fairly easy to clean. However, they are one of the most expensive flooring options, and wood can also create an echo in a space.

VINYL

You might be surprised, vinyl flooring has come a long way in recent years. It comes in a variety of styles and textures, giving you a lot of flexibility and design options. An extremely affordable flooring option, vinyl is easy to install and easy to clean. The surface, though, is highly susceptible to nicks and dents and can become loose and pop up in places over time.

LAMINATE

The benefits of laminate flooring are hard to ignore. It is also affordable, easy to install, and easy to clean. Laminate comes in a wide variety of colors and patterns and does a good job of mimicking higher-end flooring choices for a fraction of the cost. However, unlike hardwood, laminate cannot be sanded or refinished, and it shows dust and dirt more easily.

BRICK

Imagine a classic look from centuries past. Brick provides unmatched durability, it adds character and personality while helping to anchor a room's design. Brick is, however, one of the most expensive flooring options on the market and tends to absorb dirt. It's also important to remember that the mortar used between the bricks can chip and stain.

BAMBOO

This eco-friendly flooring, has quickly risen in popularity. One of the hardest floor surfaces available today, bamboo is durable, sustainable, easy to install, and easy to clean. It also adds visual integrity to a space. However, bamboo is susceptible to sunlight, scratches easily, and tends to shrink in locations with high humidity.

TILE

You have to love tile flooring's exceptional versatility, and it comes in a myriad of color choices. Tile's design possibilities are endless, it can be extremely affordable (depending on your selections), and it's easy to mix and match finishes. However, tile also chips easily, and it can be cold to walk on.

30

Area Rugs Aren't My Area. What Should I Know?

How do I determine what type of area rug to display in a room?
Should it be neutral, or does it need a pop of color? And after I've determined
the texture and pattern and color, how do I choose the correct size?

Karyn H.

KariAnne says...

Finding the perfect rug is kind of like discovering the right pair of shoes or handbag to go with an outfit. It completes the look and ties everything together. The type of rug you choose is really up to you and your room. To help you find the "just right" rug, all you need to do is size it and then style it. Here's how.

SIZE IT

Once your room design is completed—after drawing your plan onto paper (see question 42)—you can determine the correct size of rug you need for the space. Ideally, the legs of the furniture should be on the rug, and you should leave approximately 18" of open floor space between the rug and the wall. For a dining room rug, the chairs and table should be centered and placed directly on the rug. In a very large room (such as a living/dining room combo or an expansive multipurpose room), add several different rugs to the space to help establish separate "zones" within the room. Use the same measurement guidelines for the zones as you would in a separate room.

Finding the perfect rug for a room can be a full-time job. Usually, knowing what you want is the easy part. Most of the time when I imagine the design in a room, I can see the rug sitting there. It's perfect for the space—the right colors, the right pattern, the right size. It's right there in front of me. And then? I can never find the rug I imagine. It's as if it only exists in my mind. Sometimes I actually find it, but I can't afford it, it's the wrong size, or it's out of stock.

Once I found the ideal rug at the perfect price—except it was way too small for the room. So I purchased two of the small rugs. I placed them on the floor so the design matched and attached them together with a roll of carpet seam tape. It wasn't perfect. You could still see the seam just a bit, but overall it solved the problem for about half the price. After we placed the dining room table and the chairs and plates on the wall and all of the room accessories, including some amazing pillows, no one ever noticed the seam.

STYLE IT

It's easy to change out your area rugs with the seasons to freshen your spaces and create an entirely different look.

One of my go-to area rug choices is natural fiber rugs. There are many different kinds of natural fiber rugs, each with its own pros and cons. For example, sisal rugs are pretty, but they stain easily and show wear and tear. Jute rugs have an incredible texture and fun designs, but they are prone to snags and tend to unravel over time.

But seagrass? It works best in my home. Seagrass is virtually indestructible. The dirt just disappears through the woven fibers of the rug. I lift up the rug and vacuum the dirt away every so often. The kids have spilled orange soda and crushed Cheetos and Oreos on my seagrass rugs, and I just blot out the stains with a little water and they look brand-new again. The only challenge with a seagrass rug is that it's not super comfortable to walk on with bare feet—other than that, it's perfect.

Give Me Rug Rules I Can Stand On.

I'd love to decorate with rugs, but I need some guidance. Can you give me some pointers in this area?

Maggie G.

Melissa says...

When our homes feel a little uninspired, we can take a look at what we have (or don't have) beneath our furniture. Statement rugs can update the look of a room, change the mood, make a space feel much cozier and pulled together, define a conversation area, or be just the right pop of color and pattern your room needs. Who knew that a rug could accomplish so much?

A bold pattern or a bright color may seem like a risky choice, but in a more neutral space it can make the entire room spring to life. Likewise, a neutral rug can calm down more colorful and eclectic décor. Rugs are cozy and inviting. They draw people in and connect the space. Whether you prefer the simplicity of a neutral rug or the liveliness of a colorful one, rugs add texture. The organic dimensions of natural jute, a beautiful wool or silk rug, or a faux fur or animal skin rug can bring extra beauty to a room. Rugs are commonly used on wood floors, but you can also layer them over carpet—and you can even layer them over other rugs.

Most rooms with conversation areas will benefit from a rug at least 8' x 10' in size. A large room might need a bigger rug or more than one rug to define multiple functional areas of the space. A 4' x 6' or 5' x 7' can be a perfect size in entryways or smaller rooms, or next to a bed.

When you're choosing a rug to define the space, make sure you choose one large enough so that it at least fits under the front legs of each furniture piece. This unites the furniture and makes the room feel larger. Too-small rugs look lonely and lost in a room.

Use runners to brighten up a hallway or make a perfect style statement in a kitchen. Be mindful of the rug patterns in adjoining spaces, though! If you choose a lively-patterned rug for your living room, select a solid, simple stripe or natural weave for an adjoining room or hallway. Too many rugs in a similar pattern or scale can compete for attention and overwhelm a space.

If you have neutral or solid upholstery in your space, a patterned rug can be the style setter you need to give your space the "wow" factor. If a room includes statement patterns and colorful pieces, consider selecting a rug that is textured—such as sisal, jute, or seagrass—or subtly patterned. Make your rug work for you and your room. Use rugs to brighten things up or tone them down. Just as jewelry complements an outfit, a rug needs to complement the room. If you have a particularly gorgeous rug you adore, you can build the room around it—the way you would put together a great outfit around a stunning piece of jewelry.

My Mind Is as Blank as My Walls. Where Do I Start?

I'm loving my paint choices and furnishings, but my walls seem so unfinished. I have no idea what to decorate my walls with. Do you have any helpful guidelines for me?

Jordan W.

Melissa says...

Decorating the walls in your home can seem intimidating, but once you get started, you'll realize nothing is permanent (even holes in the wall can be filled, so don't let that fear hold you back!). There are ways to determine what art to display that will complement your spaces and create the feel you want. Go into the first room you plan to work on. Think through the ideas below to determine which pieces you want to include on these particular walls. Then you'll be ready to apply these ideas and enjoy your creation.

- Explore which wall hangings or pieces of framed art you already have that might work in this space. Bring them into the room and lean them against a wall. Let them be in the space for some time and see which ones are best for that room in terms of color, size, dramatic impact, etc.

- For more interest, display a variety of types and shapes of objects on the walls. Besides framed art, you can hang round baskets or even nontraditional items like a set of vintage wooden oars or a piece of driftwood.

- Practical items can become prominent wall features. Add a functional, finishing touch with a clock, a wall rack of hooks for hats and coats, a mirror, or a tiered shelf full of beautiful books.

- Pay special attention to scale. You want your displayed items to make an impact from across the room instead of being barely visible. Have the scale of one selection make sense with those of nearby pieces. For example, if you hang a large framed painting immediately above a small woven artisan basket, that dynamic will always feel top-heavy. A grouping of small objects placed just to one side of the large piece could restore balance.

- Don't feel pressure to go buy paintings if you aren't a painting kind of person. Think of all the visual elements in a room as art: the wall color, the style of your home, the amount of furniture, the colors and patterns displayed, and architectural elements such as doorways, windows, and ceiling height. Every wall doesn't have to have art.

- One bold piece of art can make a great statement in a room.

- Do you love artwork featuring quotes or words? Select a one-word art piece per room. That way the piece makes an impact, and your room won't feel as if it's shouting at you.

- Plan so that the colors that flow in your art and your furniture work together nicely. You can still have a pop of unexpected color show up in an art piece, but let the majority of colors be complementary.

- If you're still unsure if you've hit on a good balance of styles and colors, take a photo. Many of us focus on setting up individual vignettes. We decorate one wall, then go to another and put together another vignette. If the pictures all look too similar or as if they don't go together, you might want to make some changes until they look just right.

Don't worry. First, just get started. As the fun and confidence kick in, I know you will enjoy the flexibility and creativity to express yourself and your taste.

33

How Can I Have Fun with Wall Designs?

How can I replicate the creative wall designs I see in decorating magazines and blogs without a lot of experience? I'd like to try something fresh and new and add some fun patterns to my space.

Yvonne C.

KariAnne says...

If you really want to transform the look of your space, decorating your walls is a great place to start. All you need is a gallon of paint, some painter's tape, and a little imagination. And if you mess up? It's only paint. Totally fixable. Most paint projects cost under about $50 and can be completed in a weekend. All you need is a little elbow grease, patience, and imagination. So roll up your sleeves, crank up the music, and get ready to transform your space. Ready to get started? Oh good. Because your design options are endless.

STRIPES

Want one of the easiest wall treatments to create? Try stripes. They're ideal for a small space, such as an entryway, laundry room, or mudroom. They are also the perfect wall treatment to add a little personality on a tight budget.

Quick tip: Painting an odd number of stripes ensures that the same colored stripe appears on each corner of the wall.

FAUX MOLDING

Avoid the high cost of real molding with faux molding. Faux molding is an inexpensive, less permanent option than actual molding and can be added to a room in an afternoon.

Quick tip: Try faux panels, faux molding over the tops of windows and doors, faux chair rail panels, and faux picture frame molding. Life is better with a little faux.

OMBRE

For a trendy, creative option in a contemporary or modern space, try an ombre treatment. Graduated colors work with white accessories and pops of greenery.

Quick tip: You can create an ombre wall in many different styles and variations. For example, you can add the ombre treatment to three-quarters or even half of the wall, or continue the ombre color pattern onto the floor. Also consider ombre-ing the walls vertically instead of horizontally.

CHECKS

Want to add a little whimsy to a game room or craft room? Checks are a fancy, next-level first cousin to the basic stripe.

Quick tip: Take checks one step further and tape off thin vertical and horizontal stripes in contrasting colors to create a plaid wall treatment.

FAUX BRICK

Traditional brick pavers can be tricky. Faux brick is easier, a lot less messy and expensive, and the mortar always stays clean.

Quick tip: Use faux brick in a transitional room, such as a hallway or entryway. It makes a design statement, elevates a room that's often overlooked, and gives a small space a big personality.

STENCILS

When in doubt, stencils are another great option for an accent wall, especially if free-hand painted designs aren't your thing. You can purchase oversized room stencils in a variety of design styles.

Quick tip: If you don't want to paint the actual walls (or you are renting and can't paint your space), you can use fabric paint to stencil a drop cloth from the hardware store and hang it on an accent wall with dowel rods.

POST-IT NOTES

I'm totally serious here. Don't underestimate the power of a brightly colored office supply product. One of my twin daughters covered an entire wall with Bible verses and inspirational quotes written on different colored Post-it Notes. She loves her wall, and I would never change it. It's absolutely perfect for her.

34

Let There Be Light… in Each Room. But How?

I'm ready to try out different styles of lighting in my rooms, but I'm not sure how many types of lighting I can blend. Do I need lamps with matching shades, or can I have a little more freedom in my choices?

Terry D.

Melissa says…

Many people believe their lighting is fine as long as they can see what's in front of them. And a few matching shades and bases might be enough for their home. But I sense you are more like the cartoon character who has an idea lightbulb hovering above her head—ready to get creative. Follow that inspiration and include a mix of lighting types and styles in your home.

To get started, wander into each of your rooms. Take inventory. Do you have only one central light that leaves the corners dark and dreary? Your new lighting choices can do *three* amazing things for your home: Create a mood to warm up your space, illuminate task areas so you can get things done, and add personality to your décor, enhancing character, style, texture, and color.

Let's look at simple ways to accomplish these in different areas of your home. As you go through each category, mentally highlight ideas you will want to implement to light up your life.

CREATE A MOOD

Choose a variety of lamps to transform a room's mood. Yes, I'm giving you permission to break away from the floor-lamp-with-two-matching-table-lamps setup! There are so many options now.

- **Round lamps, solid lamps, and glass lamps, etc.** There are so many options. Choose what appeals to you. And don't just limit your lighting to actual lamps.

- **Wall sconces.** These are a great option to provide illumination higher up and create a lovely ambience. You can even find plug-in sconces.

- **String lights (also called fairy lights).** Aren't these pure inspiration? Some brands of string lights are battery powered. They add a warm sparkle year-round and look perfect with any season's décor.

- **And candles!** I think they are the ultimate mood lifter. Collect votive, taper, pillar, and battery-powered candles to use on candlesticks or in lanterns, hurricane jars, and non-working fireplaces.

ILLUMINATE TASK AREAS

Turning our focus to the task areas, rest assured that you can have adequate lighting sources that are cute and attractive for projects.

- **The Rx for light.** Pharmacy lamps look great tucked into corners, and you can purchase similar styles for your walls. I love desk lamps with adjustable arms to shed light where you need it.

- **Brighten small spaces.** If you're squeezed for space, look for plug-in clamp lights to place on beds, bookshelves, or dressers.

- **Don't forget the kitchen.** Often kitchens don't have adequate light for meal prep. Consider under-cabinet or rope lighting. I've also used puck-style lighting beneath cabinets for a dramatic difference.

ADD PERSONALITY

Finally, let's take a look at personality. It's often a good call to replace standard builder lighting with something that better suits your own personal sense of style.

- **Bring outdoor lighting inside.** I've displayed adorable outdoor lanterns on our staircase and entry walls.

- **Consider mixing finishes and styles.** Some of your style options include farmhouse, industrial, outdoor lanterns, antique/vintage, rustic, glam, and artistic.

- **Enjoy a lampshade refresh.** A new shade can be just the affordable touch your room needs. While white or off-white are classic options, consider a soft gray. Or go for the dramatic statement with black or colored shades. (Note: A darker shade will emit less light.) If you wander around a lighting store, you might fall in love with patterned shades. Perhaps a striped or checkered fabric would suit your style. Shades can feature a variety of trims and come in many shapes and colors, so have as much fun with styles as you want!

Ready to shop? Some of my favorite home lighting sources include Lowe's, HomeGoods, Home Depot, Restoration Hardware, Pottery Barn, Overstock, Wayfair, Target, JC Penney, World Market, TJ Maxx, Barn Light Electric, Wisteria, and IKEA, along with RH Teen and Pottery Barn Teen. And never underestimate how many unique options await being found in secondhand stores. Have fun with your lighting transformation!

35

Which Lights Complement My Space and Style?

I want to choose lighting for my home that works well with the space and the design. What are some things to consider when I head for the lighting department of my local home improvement store or the lamp section of my favorite home goods retailer?

Connie N.

KariAnne says...

Lighting is one of the most challenging areas of design in a space. I've written my blog for years, and I receive so many questions about chandeliers and pendant lights and wall sconces and floor and table lamps. What shades to use? How high to hang them? What type of lightbulb to choose for a space? Good thing I've tackled a few lighting speed bumps on my decorating journey. Here are a few tips and ideas I've learned along the way:

1 **Choose the right-sized fixture.** Nothing can underwhelm or overwhelm a room more than a fixture that's all wrong for a space.

Dining room: Measure the length of your table and then subtract 12" to determine the size of the diameter of your chandelier.

Hallways: Measure the length of the hallway and divide by 8. Typically, a light fixture is needed every 8'.

Open areas: Measure the length and width of the room and add the two measurements together. Then replace feet at the end of the sum with inches. For a 24' measurement, your light fixture should be approximately 24" wide.

2 **Layer your lighting.** Strategically placed lighting in different areas of the room ensures that you have enough light for different tasks. Installing a dimmer to your overhead light can immediately transform the look and feel of a room. A good rule of thumb is to layer in at least three different points of light in a space. Consider using a table lamp, a floor lamp, and recessed lighting or a chandelier in your living room. For the kitchen, perhaps choose a pendant light over the sink, a table lamp on the counter, and a light fixture over the kitchen table.

3 **Choose the correct bulb color.** It might seem like a small thing. I mean, after all, isn't a lightbulb just a lightbulb? Selecting the right lightbulb for the right room does make a difference. The wrong color bulb can make a room feel too cool or give an odd yellow cast to the walls. Either a warm light or a clear, bright light is the best option for most spaces.

4 **Add focus.** If you want to accent a piece of striking architecture or some fabulous wall art, a single spotlight is the best lighting choice.

5 Select the right lampshade. When you're choosing a lampshade, select one that's two-thirds the height of the base to ensure the lamp and shade have proper proportions.

Quick tip: You don't have to be limited to the lamp-and-shade combinations found in the store. Mix and match lamp bases and shades to fit your style.

6 Add bathroom lighting. The lighting fixture you select to go above the bathroom mirror should be at least one-third its width. If you're placing two fixtures in the vanity area, place them at least 28" apart to prevent shadows in the mirror. Make sure to install bright white bulbs in the bathroom to make getting ready in the morning a little easier (and a little lighter).

36

Take My Home from Dreary to Cheery and Bright.

Help! My home is lacking in natural light and feels dark and dreary, especially in the winter months. Short of knocking out some walls and adding windows, how can I remedy this?

Tina H.

Melissa says...

Good light is a benefit in any home—particularly during the cloudy, rainy months of fall and winter. Even in dark spaces, you can bring warmth to the indoors and get away from that cave-like feeling by doing a few simple things.

In a house that's lacking natural light, you're going to want to avoid dark woods and walls and even accessories that are too dark. If you need to paint all the furniture in a room white or another light color to achieve an airier look, by all means do so. Add in colors that mimic the outdoors: the blue of the sky, the white of the clouds, the green of the trees, the bright hues of the garden. As much as you can, bring the outdoors inside with colors and patterns. Adding outdoor elements—plants, flowers, shells, branches, rocks—can also give your home a brighter, outdoor feel. If you have upholstered furniture, consider using a light-colored slipcover. Even a couple of white or cream blankets draped over chairs or stacked on a bench add a pop of light.

While you can't always add in new windows on a whim or wire in new lighting at will, a few tricks can help brighten up your space. For example, here are a few ideas for your kitchen:

- Place an attractive lamp with a three-way bulb on the counter so you can use it for task lighting and for gentle light in the evening or early morning.

- Copper pots do a fabulous job reflecting the light and warmth already in the room.

- Place a large bowl or basket of brightly colored fruits and vegetables on the kitchen counter, breakfast bar, or dining table.

Sometimes a lack of natural light can be compensated for by simply adding more warm, homey touches. That's the time to bring in items that remind you that spring is on the way. Add a plant. Make a weekly trip to local farmer's markets to bring home flowers, or find inexpensive bouquets at your local Trader Joe's or another grocery store. Sometimes you just need to splurge a little to brighten your mood and get you through the winter doldrums.

Turn on all the lamps in a room, and use well-placed mirrors and glass to reflect any light that does come in. Walk around your home and notice which corners and spaces seem the darkest and least welcoming and then

add lighting to those areas. Even a small collection of battery-powered votives can brighten a dark corner and give it a cheery glow. Also, make sure your curtains are light and airy enough to let in as much natural light as possible. Sheer curtains in the fall and winter are just fine all year long if they allow you to have more light in your home. Pay special attention to your entry space. Dark entries are not very functional or inviting. A simple, small lamp or even a nightlight can create a welcoming area.

It takes some extra creativity, but additional lighting sources and little tricks can make a big difference in letting more light enter your home. And if all else fails, get outside for a little while! That's always a refreshing solution, and your home might feel just a little cozier when you come back inside and see how your little changes have added up to make a big difference.

37

Which Lights Set Which Moods?

How do I create ambience for my home with lighting?
What should I consider in various rooms?

Andrea S.

Melissa says...

One of the best kept secrets to creating a home you'll love is to pay attention to the lighting. When my husband and I were newlyweds, we lived across the street from a charming little lighting shop called Naomi's. That was where we discovered a love of lamps and lighting! We'd hunt for antique lamps at garage sales and bring them in to Naomi's to be rewired. On the weekends we'd stop in to look at new shades and unique finials (a finial is the little knob or interesting top that holds the lampshade in place) to refresh our hand-me-down lamps.

Turning on the lamps we'd collected became my favorite nightly ritual, establishing a warm and welcoming atmosphere in our home. The right lighting gives a home ambience, and the fixtures also contribute a lot toward the mood and style of a home. Some lighting blends in to support the rest of the décor, while other kinds will stand out and offer a distinct and fresh personality to the space.

Unique light fixtures can become part of your signature style. If you have dated, lackluster, or builder basic fixtures, choose something special that speaks to you. It doesn't need to be expensive. You can find statement lights for any budget! Your atmosphere will come together when your lighting does. Here are some of my favorite tricks for illuminating your favorite spaces:

- Walk around your home and note the lights, lamps, dark corners, and ambience of each room. Figure out where you most need to adjust the lighting. (Hint: Sometimes letting in light doesn't mean investing in additional light fixtures or lamps.)

- Let natural daylight into your space with undressed windows, sheer curtains, or adjustable shutters and blinds. You can also reflect and maximize light with well-placed mirrors and glass. These ideas work well in an area where you may not have access to a lot of plugs.

- Don't be afraid to choose a lamp that is larger than one you might normally consider. Remember, a lamp can be a statement piece! You can add a smaller lamp or two to the room for charm.

- Add a floor lamp to the space. I prefer small-scale, pharmacy-style metal lamps because they don't take up much room but still add a sufficient amount of light and personality.

- In an entryway, wall lamps, sconces, or a small table lamp gives a more welcoming glow.

- Overhead lights don't exactly inspire romance or rest, so don't make them your focus for lighting the bedroom. Nightstand lamps look pretty in bedrooms, and plug-in style wall sconces work well for reading in bed.

- Don't just pay attention to the hardware—look at the lighting itself too. Use the correct lightbulb for the desired effect. Light can dramatically change the color or mood of your room! Consider "warm light" bulbs for lamps and "daylight" bulbs for garages or other task areas where you need a lot of light. You can also add dimmer switches to any room for versatility.

- Add special lighting for variety and delight with string lights, hurricane lamps, chandeliers, outdoor lighting features used indoors, and candles. Think outside the box for lighting sources that add instant coziness and charm to a room.

- If you aren't yet a collector of lamps, consider becoming one. If you're starting from scratch, you can find interesting, affordable lamps at garage sales and thrift stores. You can even make your own lamps! I once made a giant lamp out of a blue glass water jug. Give yourself permission to experiment and try new things. (Make sure the lamps are safe and in good working order before you use them.)

- Every room needs at least two large lamps near the conversation area. Sometimes you can even use three or four lamps. Add another lamp or two to your gathering space to see how it makes all the difference in creating an ambience you love.

- Have you ever tried a lamp in the kitchen? Most of us use overhead lights, but it's amazing the charm a lamp on the counter adds to your kitchen space. I love to turn on my kitchen wall sconces as the sun goes down. They make the room—and my home—seem so cozy.

38

Can I Brighten My Home Without Lights?

I live in the deep, dark woods, and my house receives very little sunlight. How can I make my home seem brighter? I'm tired of turning on all the lights in the middle of the afternoon!

Missy M.

KariAnne says...

Every home comes with a unique combination of advantages and challenges. For example, a home set on the beach or in an open field—and filled with lots of big windows—might receive tons of natural light, but it can also be unbelievably hot in the summer. A house in the deep, dark woods? It's set in a gorgeous, fairy-tale location, but it can be a challenge to brighten up the space—especially in the low-light months of winter. You can, however, try a few design tricks for mimicking natural light—and save on your electricity bill in the process.

1 **Color is your best friend.** One of the best ways to brighten up a space is by painting the ceiling white. A dark ceiling—whether it's painted a dark color or paneled with wooden beams—can make the entire room seem as if it's full of shadows. Make sure your accent colors are light and bright as well. Too many dark colors are going to make a space that doesn't receive much natural light seem gloomy. When in doubt, look to nature for inspiration and decorate with the bright, light colors of spring and summer to bring the outdoors in.

2 **Choose your lamps wisely.** A bright white shade will reflect light instead of absorbing it and fill your room with light. If a bright white shade doesn't really fit your look or your décor, choose lighter shades like cream, pale yellow, or khaki instead of darker shades like navy, black, or charcoal.

3 **Mirrors add light.** Use a large mirror in your room to help reflect light. Place a mirror across the room from a light source. The light source will reflect in the mirror and create an additional "window" in your space.

4 **The type of lighting makes a difference.** One of the biggest misconceptions is to add a large overhead light to a dark room. The challenge is that a large central fixture can draw attention to the fact that the room doesn't receive much natural light by casting shadows in the space. Shadows create a harsh look to a room. Maybe consider instead a series of can lights installed in the ceiling. Can lights disperse the light throughout the space and eliminate shadows in the corners. Add a dimmer to the series of can lights to create ambiance and warmth in the room while still providing light. Spotlights on art or specific design elements in the room also bring in light without being overwhelming.

5   **Light activity areas.** Design the lighting in a room so specific activity areas have specific task light. For example, a reading corner or atop the piano needs additional lighting to illuminate certain tasks.

Finally, you could just embrace the dark and cozy look of your home. Paint the walls darker grays and charcoals and jewel-tone colors. Then add plenty of toasty throws, textured rugs, and plump pillows. Toss in a few piles of books, a stack of board games, and add dimmers to the lamps to create a moody ambiance in the room. This might be the best solution of all for a fairy-tale home set in the forest.

39

Is It Okay to Treat My Windows Differently?

What type of window treatments work best for the different rooms in my home? Also, what else should I take into consideration when deciding on curtains and shades?

Kelli R.

KariAnne says...

It's so easy to immerse yourself in the painting and the furnishing and the accessorizing and forget about the windows. All of a sudden you realize, *Wait a minute! What about the windows?* When I was decorating the rooms at my new house, the curtains were one of the last things I picked. Not because I planned it that way—I'd just overlooked them. Choosing curtains can be a little challenging. Do you go big and bold? Or will you opt for simple, classic, and clean? Having trouble choosing? Here are a few helpful guidelines for windows everywhere.

HOW TO HANG

- When considering curtains—whether full-length drapes, roman shades, or café curtains—one thing remains true: Always remember to add a little width. You don't want wimpy curtains. Extra yardage is your friend. You want your curtains to be full and luxurious, with lots of volume and a little extra fluff. A good rule of thumb for width measurement is to make sure your curtain width is two to two and a half times the width of the window. If you intend for your curtains to remain stationary, each panel should measure one and a half times the width of your window.

- Looking to hang curtains in a small space? Try swing-arm curtain rods. With these rods, the curtains are hung on the rods and then function as shutters. Swing arm rods can be mounted inside the window frame, and many come with an adjustable arm to fit the exact width of the window.

- Hang the curtain rods 5" or 6" outside the window frame to create the illusion that the windows are larger than they actually are.

WHAT TO HANG

- Not all curtains need tiebacks. Pleated curtains or hooked curtains typically hang straight down. If you do need curtain tiebacks, think outside the box. Create a tieback from a pretty bracelet or a gold link chain. You can also use a ribbon, jute twine with an industrial clasp, or a colorful scarf to hold your curtains in place.

- Unsure of what fabric to use? Here are some helpful guidelines.

    Kitchen: Lightweight cotton, usually unlined to let light in

    Dining room: Dramatic, richly textured fabrics such as velvet, linen, or silk

    Living room: Classic linen or cotton, but lined for a more formal look

    Bedroom: Casual cottons, either polished or lightweight; blackout curtains for extra privacy

    Porch: Indoor/outdoor fabrics for any space open to the elements

- Roman shades (a window treatment that consists of folds in the fabric that are layered rather than rolled up like a roller shade) are a classic, affordable option. They can be relaxed, more formal, or even fixed in place. You can install roman shades by themselves or combine them with longer curtain panels to elongate the height of a window.

- Sheer curtains are a great option if you're looking for light *and* privacy. Use a double-hung curtain rod to hang sheers directly behind your primary curtains. The sheers can be pulled across to let in the light and provide an additional layer of privacy.

40

How Do I Clothe My Naked Windows in Style?

My windows need some help getting dressed! How do you determine the appropriate style and length of curtains and drapes?

Mary C.

Melissa says...

Oh, I so relate to your windows! Trying to determine what styles will make the most of my shape and stature isn't always easy. Just like a great fitting pair of jeans or the right heels can make you feel like a new woman, windows can be dressed to elevate the style of the room, highlight their best features, or conceal a few less-than-desired elements.

Curtains are often the perfect finishing touch for a room. They can soften the look of the window and modify the infusion of light from the outdoors. Whether you use sheer curtains or velvet drapes or functional blinds, you can choose a look that's just right for your home. Here are a few tips, considerations, and guidelines for dressing windows:

1 **Evaluate.** If you're trying to determine whether to add curtains or other treatments to a window, consider the quality and design of your windows and the style of your home as well as the need for light control or privacy. If in doubt, look for an inspiration photo online that resembles your window style.

2 **Enjoy the view.** Beautiful windows, windows with views, or windows in modern-style homes may not need treatments at all, particularly if privacy is not an issue.

3 **Lengthen the look.** Installing a curtain rod a few inches or even a foot higher than the top of a window on the wall can magnify the visual impact of a diminutively sized window.

4 **Let the light in.** Ideally, panels should only cover wall space when open to maximize light.

5 **Suit your style.** Rods come in all sizes, shapes, and finishes. Not sure what style of rod to choose? Keep it simple and match the finish of your rod to other prominent finishes in your home.

6 **Personalize.** If you love details and want to add personality, select unique trim, patterns, scallops, or reversible curtains.

7 **Add some flair.** Want to get creative and embellish panels? All you need is a needle and thread (or a hot glue gun) to add trim to store-bought panels (even bed sheets and tablecloths can be transformed into one-of-a-kind curtains!).

8 **Mix and Match.** Create a custom look without a high price tag or sewing skills by pairing differing panels together. Coordinate or contrast two sets of panels for a unique look while also tying together your color scheme.

9 **Weigh the options.** Figure out your fabric needs. Heavier fabrics look more attractive when they hang all the way to the floor, and lighter fabrics are best when they're longer than floor length and "puddle," creating a soft cloud. If your curtains are too short, you can sew additional fabric to the base. And sometimes all a small window needs is a long, single panel that can be drawn back with a tie or rod.

10 **Enhance the panel.** For inexpensive options, IKEA offers long curtain panels or simple panels to customize without breaking the bank. To enhance them, add a lining to the back of the panels. So easy.

11 **Block with blinds.** Blinds are great for areas where you need to block out the hot sun or in places like the bedroom where privacy is an issue. You can even pair woven blinds or shutters with curtain panels for privacy and softness.

12 **Plan placement.** Blinds can be mounted on the outside of the window (called outside mount) or inside the window casing, depending on how much available space you have to hang them as well as the style of your trim work (or lack of trim). Be mindful of the type of windows you have and also take into consideration the impact they'll have on natural light and your view.

Bonus: The beauty of curtain fabrics can flow beyond the windows! Use curtains to shape cozy nooks around beds, benches, desks, or other furniture. Depending on your fabric choices and the setting, this outside-the-window-box thinking can create elegant or whimsical touches that suit any décor style. Kids especially love these spaces. And consider how cozy it would be to have your reading chair veiled in a color that inspires you.

41

Help Me Get a Handle on Hardware.

I want to change out the hardware on my kitchen cabinets.
Is there a "right size" for them, or should I just go with what looks good to me?

Michelle W.

Melissa says...

Changing out the hardware on your cabinets and drawers is one of the easiest, most cost-effective ways to update your look. And because it's not a big change—like new flooring or cabinetry—you have the freedom to take a few risks and have some fun.

If you are just switching out hardware, you can simplify the process by utilizing the holes already drilled for the existing knobs or pulls. For pull-style hardware, measure the distance between the two screw holes. Now you'll know the size to look for. When you plan to paint cupboards anyway, you can fill in the existing holes and start over with what you want. Whatever you do, measure and plan ahead.

There isn't a set rule for hardware dimensions, but here are my general preferences for sizing new hardware:

For drawers 18" or wider: I'd recommend two oversized knobs (1½" diameter) or one wider pull in the middle (6" to 12" from the center of one screw to the center of the other). Pulls are generally easier to use than knobs for older people or those with arthritis, so keep that in mind. For bar-style pulls, consider one that is two-thirds to three-fourths the width of your drawer.

Standard cabinets of 36" width or less: You can use a standard knob (1¼" to 1⅜") or a pull (3" to 4" wide).

Definitely trust what looks right to you—for size and style—in your space! Here are a few things to keep in mind as you finalize choices:

1   Consider your cabinet colors. A simple black-and-white palette (white cabinets with black hardware) is easy to follow and gives you freedom to mix up styles of hardware. If you've painted your cabinets a color and want that hue to take center stage, try a simpler style of hardware or make everything one style.

2   Larger spaces give you more leeway to mix finishes and have more variety. You can still get creative in a smaller kitchen, but too many materials and styles can look less eclectic and more like indecisiveness. Make sure everything at least looks as though it belongs in the same family.

3 Long bar-style pulls double as a bar for hanging towels. These are ideally situated near the sink. Bar pulls can be handy on concealed panel dishwashers or trash pull-outs.

4 Add contrast and shine to your kitchen with glass knobs. They look pretty with many styles of décor, and glass doesn't overpower other elements.

5 Select materials that are sturdy and smooth to the touch. You want them to look good *and* feel good. Before you commit to hardware for the entire kitchen, purchase a few samples and give them a trial run.

6 It's fine to play it safe. If you're unsure, go ahead and match the cabinet hardware finishes to your kitchen faucet. Consider choosing two finishes that complement your kitchen: for instance, brushed nickel with glass finishes. Also take into consideration any exposed hinges.

7 If you want to get creative, go for it! I've used a mix of modern satin nickel bin pulls, brass and mother-of-pearl round knobs, and mercury glass square knobs. Combining metals such as silver and gold makes the kitchen feel more timeless. I even added an oil-rubbed bronze hook and two brass animal knobs (a fox and a bunny) to the drawers of a free-standing stock island to give it a quirky personality. If your budget is tight, you can even paint existing knobs in new colors. Feel free to make a fun statement!

Furniture & Space Planning

Arranging furniture in rooms can be a real puzzle. How much open space should you leave? What are the rules about where to place sofas, chairs, end tables, and coffee tables? How can you make a giant room look cozy or how can you keep a small room from appearing too cluttered? Every home has its own creative design, and each room provides us with its own unique set of challenges.

The key? Having fun with your furniture and creating a warm, welcoming space where friends and family gather, chat, laugh, pray, and draw closer together. You'll learn how to design different corners of your home for different activities, such as creative pursuits or rest and relaxation, and you'll discover how to decorate and organize those spaces in a way that's just right for you.

Whether you're starting from scratch with a brand-new home or reimagining well-loved furnishings in your longtime abode, you'll be inspired to achieve a look that truly makes your house feel like a home.

42

How Do I Plan My Furniture Placement?

I need some guidelines for furniture placement in various rooms. I'm completely clueless when it comes to space planning and visualizing how everything will look. Do I just bring everything in and hope it will fit—or is there a better way?

Missy A.

KariAnne says...

There's nothing quite as exhilarating—or as exhausting—as planning out your space. You don't want to rush the planning or skip it. Remember the old saying, "If you fail to plan...you plan to fail." Planning your space is a lot like wearing Spanx to your high school reunion—it's absolutely necessary. It's so easy to be all about shopping and thrifting and creating and decorating and overlook the planning part. Or maybe you might have some vague idea of a plan that isn't completely formed or decided on. Truth? A little planning can help you achieve your desired look for your home, prevent furniture heartbreak, and save you a few pennies (or hundreds of dollars) along the way.

1 **Measure.** My number one tip is to measure, measure, and measure again. Start with the overall dimensions of the room—the length, the width, and the height of the space. Then, using a pencil, mark these room dimensions on graph paper. Next, draw the lines of your room to scale on the paper and write down the length of each wall. These measurements will help you determine if your furniture will fit. Be sure to keep a record of all your room dimensions for future projects in a planning notebook.

2 **Outline.** You're not quite ready to start adding furniture yet. First, you need to note on your plan what is permanent to the spaces. On the graph paper, mark the electrical outlets, light switches, windows, and doors in the rooms. Also include any permanent fixtures the rooms have, including pillars, fireplaces, wood stoves, closets, and built-ins.

3 **Anchor.** This part is a little like planning your dollhouse. Sketch or print out miniature paper furniture pieces to represent the items you own (or would like to purchase) for the spaces. Now you're ready to start moving these pieces around the detailed outline of the rooms you penciled in on your graph paper. Begin with the largest piece of furniture in each room. For example, this might include the couch or sectional in the living room, the dining table in the dining room, and the bed in each bedroom. These pieces function as the anchors for each room.

Quick tip: Many times you'll want the piece—such as the couch or bed—to face the entrance to the room.

4 Arrange. Now that you've determined your anchor pieces, add in additional elements—chairs, sofa tables, coffee tables, rugs, lamps, hutches, large plants, bookshelves, and other accent pieces to your plan. It's a good idea to place the furniture away from the walls. Bringing the furniture into the room creates a warm, welcoming space. Be sure to design for comfort. Each seating area needs an adjoining surface for people to set down drinks, books, and other items. You will also want to ensure there is adequate lighting in each room. Tuck ottomans and poufs under tables for extra seating, and add oversized baskets next to chairs for storing throws and additional pillows. Now your room is ready for its new design.

43

Any Tips for Arranging Furniture?

I'd love some advice on furniture arrangement. Many blogs and magazines show rooms from varying angles, but we never get to see the entire room. What are some general guidelines for arranging my furniture?

Barbara J.

Melissa says...

Rooms come in all different sizes and styles and serve a variety of purposes, but when it comes to rooms where people live and gather—living rooms, family rooms, multipurpose rooms, even outdoor porches and living spaces—you can follow a few general guidelines.

1 **Assess the space and the function.** In a room where people gather together, be careful that your furniture isn't separated in such a way that it's difficult to have a conversation. You don't have to shove the sofa and chairs together, but you should establish a conversation area that's close enough so you don't need to shout at the top of your lungs to be heard. If you're arranging furniture in a particularly large space, you can still follow the same rule. You just need to create more groupings. Just as we need friends, so does our furniture! If you're having trouble communicating, it might not be you. It might just be that your furniture is too far apart.

2 **If you feel a room isn't as cozy or as functional as you want it to be, move the furniture around.** If you have all the pieces up against the wall, bring a few of those pieces into the room's primary space. This added dimension will shift a room that feels as if it's always prepped for someone to come in and clean the floors into an inviting, gathering place.

3 **Tending to functional solutions will ultimately create a better room.** Make sure you have plenty of surface area next to your seating for people to set down a book, a cup of coffee, or creative projects such as knitting or drawing. Try not to block the windows so you can take full advantage of natural lighting. Can a person reach the outlet that is behind the recliner?

4 **If a room seems too crowded, remove a piece or two.** Remember, you need some breathing space. If something seems too bulky for a room, it probably is. How do things look now? Keep assessing and rearranging until it feels right. (If people start hanging out more in that room, it's a good sign your changes are working!)

Sometimes all it takes is moving one piece of furniture. I have a glass-door cabinet I used to have in the living room, but it just didn't feel right. So I moved it to the bedroom—even though I'd previously determined the piece would be too big for that space. I'm so glad I made the switch because I loved it there! Without that cabinet on the wall of the living room, I was free to try a new arrangement. After a few attempts, I discovered the perfect setup—it was inviting, and it fully incorporated our window's view as the main focal point.

5   **Be Goldilocks.** Before and after you move furniture pieces around, sit in each chair for a few minutes to get a sense for how it feels. So many of us end up in our favorite perches in our own home that we forget to experience a space from another vantage point.

This is extremely helpful to do. You'll notice which places feel disconnected. You'll identify that the ottoman is at an odd angle or that a bookcase blocks a person's line of sight. And you might solve a mystery, like why the dog always trips on the way to his bed: because the floor vent makes the rug corner curl up. Who knows what you will discover!

Rearranging your furniture is one of the most inexpensive and dramatic ways to get a new look for your home. All it requires is a little temporary havoc and some experimentation. Eventually you'll hit on an arrangement that's ideal for your home, and you'll be happy you took the time to shuffle things around until you found your perfect fit.

Can I Arrange Furniture Creatively Inside the Box?

What is the best way to arrange furniture in my living/dining rooms? The space isn't fancy—
basically just a rectangular box with a front door that opens right into the living area.
How can I give it some character and charm?

Sandra V.

KariAnne says...

Classic spaces like these are a great foundation to build on. In addition to furniture arrangement, the key to creating character and charm is adding in warmth and texture with textiles and accessories.

- Before you start, keep in mind that your furniture should fill about two-thirds of your room. If you have too much furniture in a space, it's hard to move around. But if you don't have enough furniture in the room, it appears somewhat unfinished and not very welcoming. When planning your room arrangement, make sure to include fireplaces, cabinets, oversized furniture, and anything else that takes up space in your room in your formula.

- Next, designate areas of the space for separate functions. For example, add a small console table next to the front door and some hooks and hangers to define an entryway. Define separate living and dining areas with area rugs. Group chairs, tables, and bookshelves to add interest and functionality to the space.

- In an open concept space with a combined living and dining room area, establish a central focal point for each room. A fireplace, a picture window, or a striking piece of furniture works well in the living room. A sparkling chandelier, a brilliant painting, or even a unique table can take center stage in the dining room.

- After arranging the furniture, layer in furnishings and accessories. Have fun with colors and patterns and textures. In addition, adding greenery to a room adds an organic element and brings a space to life.

- If your budget allows, additional crown molding, chair rails, built-ins, or a window seat all work together to add character and make a space feel unique.

- Keep it simple. Resist the urge to overdecorate a space. You don't need to cover your dining room table and bookcases with knickknacks. Instead, reduce clutter and select accessories and furniture you truly love. Allowing a room to breathe makes guests immediately feel at home in a space and creates purposeful design.

Does a TV Have to Take Over a Room?

How do you decide on a focal point for a room? For instance, I want the focal point to be the fireplace, but my husband wants it to be the TV. Which actually serves as the best choice? Help!

Leslie B.

Melissa says...

Determining an appropriate furniture arrangement around conflicting focal points is a common dilemma. Before you and your husband end up facing opposite directions, let's take a look at the big picture:

1   **What is the purpose of your room?** Determining the purpose of the room will help you arrange your furniture. Furniture should be placed so it serves the needs of people who will be in the space. Will it primarily be a room for entertainment, gathering, or quiet times of reading and talking? Or will it host a combination of activities? If you and your husband have differing views on how this space will be used, design the room so it serves multiple needs in an attractive way.

2   **Where can you put a TV so it's easy to view but doesn't become a statement?** We're fortunate that today's technology has produced TVs more easily incorporated in a room's décor. If your TV is used on a regular basis, it makes sense to arrange the key furniture pieces so everyone watching feels comfortable. Rooms are for living, after all. And many rooms are multipurpose. It's possible to create a design compromise that serves various needs without awkward furniture arrangement.

- If the TV can be placed next to the fireplace, you'll be able to arrange the furniture so people are gathered around both.

- Placing a TV above a fireplace allows you to view the TV and enjoy the fireplace at the same time. Test the viewing angle for comfort first.

- If you don't like the impact of a blank screen or a black box on the wall, shop for a TV that can display artwork or family photos.

- If you need to place the TV on an opposing wall from a fireplace, get creative with furniture arrangements. It may be possible to set a couple comfortable chairs facing the fireplace while the sofa is directed toward the TV. Or add swivels to club chairs so they can turn toward the TV for movie time.

- Reduce the TV's prominence. Paint the wall around the TV a darker tone or incorporate a wall-mounted television into an art grouping.

- Have the TV inset in an attractive cabinet that becomes the backdrop element for conversation times.

KariAnne has a great example of how the television can be visible but not take over the room. Notice how she created a focal point with a gallery wall over the couch that draws your eye away from the TV.

3 **Rearrange until a design creates a focal point and reinforces the right mood and purpose.** Keep in mind that the first thing your eye is drawn to in a room doesn't have to be a TV or a fireplace. A focal point can be any *statement piece* that draws attention in a room because of its color, shape, style, size, element of surprise, or detail. It might be just one object—like a gorgeous piano or a large picture window—or a grouping of things—like an antique bookcase with a few cozy armchairs.

In one of my rooms, the focal piece was an antique bookcase that made you want to settle down with a good book for the afternoon. Even better? That one piece of furniture solved both the issue of the purpose—a room to read and study in—*and* the focal point. I'm not always that clever, but it's nice when it works!

Create a room that draws people together and invites them in with a visually impactful and welcoming statement.

46

How Do I Size Up My Furniture Upgrades?

I have some rooms that desperately need furniture, and now
I have the money in my budget to purchase them, but I'm not sure what size
pieces to buy for my space. Can you give me some general guidelines?

Suzi B.

KariAnne says...

Furniture is something you want to get *right*. It's not like a pillow that can be tossed in a different area or a painting that can find another wall if it's the not the right size. You're either going to be spending a lot of time refinishing or reupholstering it or a lot of money on a new piece of furniture, so you want to make sure you get your dimensions right before you make the commitment.

Measuring your space is essential. (Total decorating aside: refer to question 42 for additional information on this.) I can also give you some general guidelines for furniture placement and size considerations. Be sure to adjust for the traffic patterns in your individual space when placing your furniture.

- Arm heights of the sofa and chairs in the room should be approximately the same height.

- Allow a distance of 36" between the dining room table and the walls of the room. Allow a distance of 36" between the dining room table and the edge of the rug.

- Allow 24" from the edge of the area rug to the walls of a room.

- Allow 10" of clearance for traffic flow between the sofa and armchairs.

- Allow a distance of 18" from the edge of the sofa to the coffee table.

- Be sure to measure the dimensions of a larger piece of furniture, such as a sofa or table or hutch, and mark it on the floor with painter's tape before purchasing any new pieces for the room. This step will help you visualize the size of a piece and make sure it's a good fit for the space.

- If you don't have the space for it, don't try to make it work. A living room doesn't *have* to have a sofa if it doesn't fit. A couple of comfortable chairs will work just as well, and you can choose something else for your focal point—such as a big, bold mirror or a gallery wall. Work with what you have.

- If space is a little tight, choose round or oval tables instead of square or rectangle pieces. They add a little more room to your design plan.

- Ideally, a coffee table should be about two-thirds as wide as your sofa.

- Make sure that beds don't overpower a room. A king-sized bed may be ideal, but if a queen or full fits better in the space, choose that option. To create a calm atmosphere, bedrooms need plenty of breathing room.

- Before you attempt to move oversized furniture from one floor to another, make sure the pieces will actually clear the stairs or the corners or the entrance to the room. Measure sizes. Check heights. Those helping you move the furniture will thank you (and so will your furniture and walls and door frames).

47

What Tips Maximize an Open Floor Plan?

Open floor plans are popular right now, but I'm struggling to coordinate those rooms. I want each room to have its own purpose and personality, but the spaces need to flow together too. How can I strike a balance?

Maria B.

Melissa says...

When rooms truly flow together, you can be in one room and look through it to another space without feeling jarred by something that looks wrong, undone, or awkwardly in the way. You can achieve this by starting with the big elements—walls and floors—and coordinate them so they look pleasing and connected. It is very doable! Plan these elements to be complementary throughout the area, and then the individual spaces can still have their own personality.

CREATE COLOR CONTINUITY

In an open floor plan with connecting walls, I recommend painting with one cohesive neutral color. This will simplify the backdrop, make the walls easier to paint, and allow you to focus on other ways to bring a new look to each space.

To give each room a unique personality, find a spot to introduce more color or tie in one from an adjoining room. For example, if your walls are painted a soft neutral gray in a connected living, kitchen, and dining room, you could add yellow barstools in the kitchen for a cheery pop of sunshine or paint your island a deep navy blue. Then in the next room, a connected dining room, you could hang a large framed botanical artwork featuring green vines with blue or yellow to tie in the kitchen. Then in the living room

on the other side of the dining room, you could create a more dramatic or moody atmosphere with a deep gray rug or a navy velvet sofa. Then bring in plants or pillows to subtly tie into the green of the botanical art in the connected dining room. Common colors woven throughout an open space will lead the eye with ease.

Another option is to paint adjoining rooms in shades of the same color or color family. As long as there's an appropriate spot to make the color switch, you can vary your paint color. Stick to a palette of either warm tones or cool tones for a cohesive look between spaces.

My favorite paint trick to is to create a visually interesting but not jarring color transition by simply adding various percentages of white to lighten a deeper hue. Shades of the same base color will create a beautiful and effortless flow between adjoining rooms. Experiment with this, as it works better with some paints than others.

DESIGNATE WITH RUGS

Rugs will help reduce the sound that travels in an open floor plan, and they also are a perfect way to designate each distinct room. Take your time selecting the rugs you want. Be sure the one you choose to anchor the living area doesn't clash with the one that is anchoring the dining area since both would be in view. Complementary color tones or patterned rugs will offer interest. If both rugs have a pattern, I would recommend selecting one in a larger scale and one in a smaller scale.

DISTINGUISH WITH ARCHITECTURE

You can design beautiful distinctions between connected spaces with added architectural detail. Beams or millwork can be installed to highlight various ceiling heights or special spaces within an open floor plan. Wall treatments, such as wood paneling or patterned wallpaper, can create interest. Built-in benches or bookcases add character while offering a useful separation between spaces.

Let the open room design become your pass to freedom rather than an obstacle. Experiment, move things around, and adjust. You'll find yourself with a natural plan that works well with your home and your own personal style.

We created continuity in our open floor plan with hickory flooring throughout. Here, we created a distinct separation between the kitchen and living room using both architectural details and furniture placement.

48

I'm Open to Ideas to Fill Open Spaces.

I just moved from a very small home to a very large home. I'm used to small-space decorating, but now I'm stumped! How can I decorate a large, open living space with long walls?

Julie K.

Melissa says...

Your new home will be fabulous for entertaining, but the real trick is making those larger-than-average rooms cozy and functional for day-to-day living. Your existing furniture most likely looks out of scale and sparse in the new living space.

I truly understand this dilemma! For several years we lived in a big home with rambling spaces. In fact, that house felt so large I occasionally found myself taking long walks to exercise and would revisit rooms I hadn't been to in months! I began to realize that those spaces were unused not because they couldn't be useful, but because they were not as warm, comfortable, or inviting as they could have been.

So trust me when I say that you will feel much better about decorating your large rooms and more confident when you rein in the visuals and create some comfort and proportion in your primary spaces. Here are my favorite tips for styling a bigger living room:

1 **Designate zones.** Small living rooms likely only have room for one conversation area, but large rooms can function as so much more. Create several functional areas within the room, such as a conversation zone (or two or three!), a media zone, an area for a writing desk, a console or a game table, a dining area, or perhaps a reading area.

2 **Divide the space visually.** You can add ceiling beams, half walls, or pillars to divide up a room visually in semipermanent ways, or you can use area rugs, curtains, wallpaper, and furniture placement to create cozy spaces within the larger room. A sofa with its back to another space, a chaise lounge, a large bench, tables between chairs, an attractive screen, large lamps, or plants can also help divide the room into specific areas.

3 **Anchor the room.** A sectional, a large sofa, a large coffee table, or even built-in bookcases or a piano will help anchor a room so smaller pieces can be tucked in here and there as accents if necessary.

4 **Lighten things up.** Choose lamps of larger scale with similar shades and then mix in slimmer, less obtrusive metal floor and wall lamps to bring lighting all around the room. A lack of ambient and task lighting will make the conversation areas, corners, and even walls in large rooms feel empty, cold, and uninviting.

5 **Use color.** Color and pattern can be used to break up big expanses of walls. Add wainscoting with varying shades of neutrals or colors painted above and below the molding. For high ceilings, paint the ceiling a shade or two or even several shades darker than your walls to make the room feel snugger and cozier.

6 **Avoid too much wall hugging.** With a larger room, you can pull seating out from the walls to create a much cozier conversation area around a focal point like a fireplace. And don't fear empty walls! More space means more versatility. You can use wall space for art, buffets and consoles, benches, bookcases, or additional conversation areas.

7 **Layers cozy up the space.** If the room feels cold, sound echoes, or it just doesn't seem cozy, you might need more layers. Add area rugs (you can even layer two rugs together), hang curtains, bring in some baskets, and display a few more fun accessories to personalize the room. Softer spaces seem more inviting, so be sure to include plenty of upholstered pieces along with pillows and blankets.

8 **Repeat, repeat, repeat.** The more furniture and accessories you display, the more haphazard a room can feel. Tie a large room of furniture together and unify your style through repetition. Repeating fabric patterns or colors on chairs or throw pillows will help carry your eye around the room and feel visually more pleasing.

49

I Want a Bedroom Makeover (Without Losing Sleep Over Money).

I have a limited budget to redo my master bedroom. How would you recommend
I prioritize my projects to have the most impact on my space?

Barb S.

KariAnne says...

A limited budget might seem like a major problem, but it can be a blessing in disguise. When you know exactly how much (or how little!) you have to spend, you're able to prioritize your projects and focus on the ones that will really make a difference. You can also figure out how to save on certain items so you can afford one or two splurges.

Clearly, the focal point of your bedroom—and the place where you spend the most time—is the bed itself. Are you satisfied with the current size and state of your bed? This isn't a small purchase, so it's totally going to depend on how much money you have to work with, but a brand-new bed could be well worth it. If you don't necessarily need a king or queen size, go with a double (also called a full). This will save you quite a bit. Consider whether you want a mattress or a futon (which will dictate what type of frame you buy). You can also boost up the comfort of an existing mattress with a mattress topper.

You're going to want to purchase the highest-quality sheets you can. Consider your favorite type of material. Do you need 100 percent cotton? Are you a fan of flannel sheets in the winter? Even if you need to invest in several sets, the good news is you can always find sales or good deals. I keep my bedding simple. White and khaki with a down comforter and a duvet cover from IKEA. And look for flannel sheet sets during those post-Christmas sales. Invest in a comforter or duvet cover you really and truly love. (Remember, you can find these for a good price!) Then add in coordinating throws and decorative pillows you discover at a discount home goods store. Have a photo of your comforter on your phone so you can always check to see if accessories will match. And don't stress out about a perfect match—close enough is just fine if the items are the right style.

Beyond the bed, you can find furnishings and accessories for any budget.

- When I needed inexpensive bedroom curtains, I went with drop cloths straight from the aisle of the home improvement store. Simple and neutral, they look like linen (if you squint a little). I hung them up with clip-on rings.

- You can reclaim an armoire from a yard sale or from another room in your house.

- Try a seagrass rug. Simple and sturdy, it will continue to look great over time.

- It's also easy to find, refinish, and repaint bedside tables. Just add a few books, a lamp, a mason jar of flowers, and maybe a cute little photograph in a frame. Done.

Really, you don't require a lot in the bedroom. As long as it's restful and brings you joy, that's all you need.

50

How Do I Make the Best of My Empty Nest?

My last child is leaving home, and I'm about to have an empty nest. I'm planning to turn her room into my own space for doing artwork, exercise, and hosting overnight guests. Is it possible to make this room (which isn't very big) workable and cute at the same time?

Kathy M.

Melissa says...

Changes in life always bring about different needs for organization. You can make it work—and yes, you can make it cute too. Creating a room that fulfills more than one purpose is like putting together a puzzle, and it's one of my favorite things to do. The key is to not become overwhelmed...you want to enjoy the new possibilities for your space. To figure out how the puzzle pieces best fit together, spend time refining and problem solving.

- Freestanding furniture takes up a lot of space, so see if you can eliminate pieces of furniture by utilizing built-ins. Without a lot of furniture in your way, you're free to move things around and use the room for a variety of purposes. You will get excited about the new vision.

- If you're using the room for occasional overnight guests, you'll need plenty of good storage for art supplies, exercise equipment, and anything else that doesn't need to be accessed by guests. Storage ottomans, under-the-bed drawers, a built-in window seat with storage underneath, a long built-in cabinet under the windows with compartments to stash stuff—all of these will help open up space while providing you with storage options.

- A sofa with a pull-out bed for guests helps keep the room from looking like a thrown-together guest room, especially when you're in the midst of art projects. If you don't have space for side tables or lamps, you can add sconces to bring light to the space. When it comes to decorations, think fun but functional. I used an oversized clock in a multipurpose room as a quirky focal point that also served a purpose. The secret to success is creativity and strategic planning.

- If you have a closet in the room, try not to use it as a hiding place for items before guests arrive. Remember, your guests will need ample open space for their suitcases and personal belongings. Add a handy storage chest or cabinet to the closet for extra blankets or towels, provide some hangers, and place a few toiletries on top of the chest or cabinet. When the room is not in use as a guest room, this will keep you from piling extra stuff in the closet—and it will make it easy to get ready for arriving guests.

- Allow the room to keep its new identity. Preserve it even when it's tempting to use the space for other types of storage, which is easy to do in a space that doesn't always get daily use. Resist the habit of piling things in the "extra" room—until suddenly you realize those piles are out of control! You want the room to keep its new function and not become crowded and cluttered with items that belong elsewhere or need to be tossed.

- Finally, keep going through the space. Which art supplies have seen better days? Are you really using all those pieces of exercise equipment? Do you need to bring in some cute new storage containers that serve the dual purpose of housing items and adding to your décor?

As your family changes and your interests and needs shift, you and your home will benefit greatly from these seasons of reorganizing. Have fun, and allow your creative juices to flow!

51

How Can I Love My Kitchen Again?

I'm so tired of my dated kitchen that I don't even want to spend time in it anymore! I don't have a large budget, but what are some quick and easy ways I can upgrade the space?

Kathy E.

KariAnne says...

No household project strikes fear into the heart—and the wallet—like a kitchen remodel. Even if your kitchen is dated and ugly, you need it. You can't just close the door and pretend it doesn't exist anymore. (And anyway, sometimes there isn't a door you can close.) So let's just dig right in and deal with it. Experience is often the best instructor, and I have plenty of that. When you're immersed in a remodel, and things that were supposed to cost $2.00 ended up costing $2.50, all those 50-cent additions…well, they add up! Consequently, my kitchen budget was cut in half. Gone were the marble countertops. Gone was the built-in kitchen island. Gone were the custom cabinets. It was just me and a stack of laminate countertop samples. And now? Years later as I look at my kitchen? I'm so happy. Because when you remodel a kitchen and the funds are low and you're wondering if your five-gallon paint bucket can be repurposed as a sink, you only need one thing: a little imagination.

- If you can't afford natural stone countertops, embrace the laminate. There are so many great options for laminate countertops, including different finishes and edges. Some of the best options mimic granite or natural stone or (my personal favorite) marble. You can just pretend you have the real thing.

- I wanted a custom-built kitchen island. I also wanted to be Miss America when I was younger. Neither plan worked out. But what I ended up with was so much better (well, on the kitchen front). The kitchen island I bought was only $399 from IKEA. Eight years later, it still looks like new. The shelves are covered with a stainless steel liner, and the island has a butcher-block countertop and a place for stools on the other side. And it's exactly what I needed at a price that fit my budget.

- I really wanted cabinets with glass doors, but they were super expensive. So I added my own. I ordered the shell of the cabinets to match the other cabinets we were installing. Then I ordered the glass door fronts from a local cabinet maker. It was literally almost half the cost. And that little row of glass-paneled cabinets? It makes my inexpensive cabinets look extra custom.

- To make my kitchen more interesting but still save money, I added in my own architectural features. I painted brick and created a recipe wall with a plate rack that we built on a blank wall. And I installed new decorative door molding. And faux transom windows in the space. All it took was paint, caulk, simple molding pieces, and a little direction.

- Finally, I really wanted to put cabinets on one of the kitchen walls, but that was going to be too expensive. Like, way-out-of-our-budget expensive. So I found a kitchen hutch at a yard sale for less than $100, which accomplished the same purpose for one-sixteenth the price. I'm satisfied with it. In fact, I'm more than satisfied. I think it looks better and a little more farmhouse.

Never underestimate the blessing of a limited budget and the beauty of a little imperfection.

52

What Makes a Small Space Extra Inviting?

I need help decorating my tiny living room! I have no full walls and the space is too small to float furniture, but I want to make it cozy and inviting. How can I accomplish this?

Anne J.

Melissa says...

Oh, I love the challenge of finding small-space solutions! It's tricky sometimes, but it's actually kind of fun to figure out the answers to decorating dilemmas in a cozier house. Now is the time to think creatively—on a small scale—to clear out what's unnecessary and bring in the charm.

PLAN THE SPACE

- If possible, start with an empty room so you can assess the architecture of the space. Look at the ceiling, the walls, and the floors. Every surface matters! Give the room a fresh coat of paint, consider adding wall or ceiling treatments, built-in cabinets, and millwork, or installing new flooring. The right backdrops can envelope a small space in charm even before you've added furnishings.

- Make sure every item you bring into the room contributes something of value to the space. Small rooms can't handle a lot of clutter.

- A small-scale armoire could hold books, a laptop, and photos in decorative frames.

- Plan ahead and look for desks or tables that have pull-out extenders for those times when you need a little more room.

EMBRACE A MOOD

- Focus on playing up the ambience of the room with lighting, comfortable pieces, and inviting textures to enhance the look you're going for without taking up extra space.

- Look for a cozy rug. If you are rearranging or getting new furniture, putting a rug in the room first will make the rest of the experience less of an aerobic exercise.

- Accent lighting will make small spaces inviting, so tuck in lamps, twinkle lights, and candles (battery operated for safety).

AIM FOR FUNCTION

- Take care not to clutter the space with too much free-standing furniture. Built-ins can make a world of difference in how a small room feels and functions.

- Two smaller tables can be more versatile and less overwhelming than one big coffee table. Round tables can make navigation less cumbersome in tight quarters.

- Search for attractive and appropriately sized containers and baskets to organize items inside, which makes your room look cozier as well as tidy. When a small room feels comfortable but organized, you are much more likely to keep it that way.

- Accent tables that have fold-down leaves can be charming and free up more floor space and can be opened up as needed.

- Use ottomans with storage space to corral clutter and provide extra seating for guests.

The great thing about a small room is it's already cozy by nature, so have fun playing it up and making the most of every square inch.

53

Can I Distress Furniture Without Stress?

I love the farmhouse look, and I also want to start DIYing some of my own furniture pieces.
I'd like to start with a table as a fun and functional anchoring piece.
Do you have any hints or helps? I really like the distressed look.

Jenny B.

KariAnne says...

Farmhouse style and a fun and functional DIY project? Come sit by me. And the best part? A table is a great place to start. It's a great anchor piece in any dining room, living room, or even back porch. Clean your table thoroughly and then take a closer look at your yard sale find. Check for repairs that need to be made, sand rough edges, and remove hardware before starting any project.

One of my favorite DIY projects is a farmhouse table I created for my back porch. The entire cost of the project was only $10.97. It started off a little rough around the edges, but now? I would marry that table if I could. Or at least take it to Vegas to watch the Elvis impersonators sky-dive. When I found it, the top was warped and the paint was peeling. It looked forlorn and sad and more than a little neglected. I took it home and transformed it in an afternoon. Here are the details for the project:

1. **I started with a coat of white paint with primer.** I let that dry and then added a second coat.

2. **I bought a 24" x 48" piece of thin plywood.** I measured and went with a piece slightly larger than the dimensions of the table.

3. **I cut the plywood.** I measured and then cut approximately 4" strips of wood. (You can have the people at the home improvement store cut it for you.)

4. **Then I glued the plywood to the table top.** I used wood glue for this. I know, right? It was as simple as glue.

5. **Last, I stained it with Provincial stain.** After applying my favorite stain, I let it dry before sealing it with polyurethane.

If you love the distressed look, it's super easy to achieve that effect as well. You can take a $5 find and make it look like a million dollars. Here's another simple DIY project:

1. **Start by choosing your table wisely.** The lines and details on a table can totally make or break the finish. Look for one with curves and legs that make a statement and edges you can sand.

2. **Prime the table.** If you hear nothing else from this DIY, DO NOT skip this step—please. You don't know what was put on the table before. You don't know

what finish you are starting with. Priming transforms all that history into a blank slate.

3 **Paint the table.** Work with a neutral or a color that fits your design.

4 **Dry brush with white acrylic craft paint.** This step is easy, but it takes a little practice. Don't use too much paint. Instead, you want your brush to be somewhat dry (hence the term *dry brush*). Take the brush and lightly drag it across the table top in the SAME DIRECTION. If your paint lines don't go in the same direction,

your table won't look distressed—it will just look messy. Let the paint dry.

5 **Then dry brush burnt umber craft paint.** Again, go lightly with this step.

6 **Sand it.** Last, take a piece of 60-grit sandpaper and lightly sand the edges of the piece and anywhere there is a raised edge. Then take a tack cloth and remove any excess wood dust before sealing the entire piece with a coat of acrylic sealer. Your yard sale find is now a masterpiece.

54

Help Me Mix and Match Without a Mishmash!

Can you give me some general guidance for pulling everything together and making my space work for me? I love to mix and match colors and patterns and furniture styles, but I'm afraid my eclectic mix of furnishings is just going to look weird.

Leslie B.

KariAnne says...

Sometimes decorating wisdom shows up when I least expect it. Like when the twins and I watched *Cinderella* for the 5,216th time. I wasn't planning on sitting down. I wasn't planning on watching. I already knew how it ended. But when those imploring blue eyes looked up at me, I plopped down with a cup of coffee and watched the movie one more time. There's always something new to learn. There's always a little bit of life wisdom to discover along the way. Here are some truths I learned from Cinderella that apply to our lives as the primary designers of our homes:

1   Be kind. Especially to animals and the family who lives in your house. Their needs are important too. Your cat or dog is also a member of your family. Set up a cozy pet bed in your favorite space. Add a cute cover that blends with your décor. If your daughter wants to display her hand-painted rock collection right by your front door, give her permission to decorate. It's her home as well. Her creations say, "Welcome" so much more than a trendy mat or a garden gnome.

2   Have courage. If you look at the pieces you want to display, sometimes all you see is a hodgepodge of colors and patterns and styles that don't exactly go together. But that's the beauty of creating something from nothing. Be bold. Go ahead and put that brand-new sofa next to the two thrift shop chairs you recently refinished. Just layer in some coordinating pillows to add an element of cohesive design.

None of the tables in your living room match each other in style? No worries. Simply paint them all the same color and add vases full of flowers. Have the courage to use what you have and pull the unexpected together.

3   Know how to rock a bad hair day. And a sooty face. And a torn gown. In other words, don't rule out pieces that are imperfect. That gorgeous chair you found at the yard sale that has chips? Those add character to the piece. The bookshelf that's perfectly functional except for the hole in the top? Cover it with a cute tray. Those dining room chairs—the ones collected over time that kind of, sort of look as if they go together? They do—because they are part of YOUR design.

4 **Always help others in need.** That includes your furniture and your rooms. If the bedroom looks a little sparse and could use a little extra help, borrow a piece of furniture from another room. Shopping your house is one of the easiest ways to freshen your spaces.

5 **Be true to who you are.** This is perhaps the most important piece of decorating advice as well as an important life lesson. You are unique. And special. And brilliant. And so is your home. If your eclectic mix of furnishings is really and truly *you*, it is totally going to work when you pull it all together.

Color, Paint, & Patterns

When planning your design for your room, making color choices (and committing to them) can be a little overwhelming. Just walk into a paint store and look at the variety of available options. Even one shade—mint blue or sunny yellow—comes in what seems like a zillion different options. Or wander into a fabric store with the intention of choosing three or four coordinating patterns to make pillow covers. You thought about choosing a floral and maybe a solid or a stripe, but soon twenty or thirty bolts of fabric have caught your eye—and you love them all.

Even if you have a well-defined idea of what you like, coordinating a color palette can be a real challenge. How do you balance hues trending right now with shades that speak to you? What about choosing colors to match the style and era of your home and existing architectural features you *can't* change?

With a little know-how and some basic design principles, you can kick all that overwhelming to the curb and gain the confidence you need when it comes to coordinating an inspiring and relaxing look for your home.

55

Is There a Secret to Planning Color Schemes?

Can you provide some guidance when it comes to paint colors and schemes—both interior and exterior? I want to coordinate my home's look, but I'm not sure where to start.

Heather F.

Melissa says...

Paint color is a great place to start when adding your personal stamp of style to your home. I want to dispel one decorating myth right away: Dark paint in a room doesn't have to mean dreary or depressing. While you can simplify choices with whites and monochromatic paint schemes—using all light tones for a soft, airy look—it's also fun to go for the dramatic effect of moody tones. Mixing things up with deeper shades of painted walls or accessories can bring a lot of drama, coziness, and personality to a space.

A simple way to create impact with color is to stick with an essentially neutral room and then spice things up with a pair of boldly colored chairs or accessories. Or you can paint a door black or deep green or dark blue for an arresting pop of color in an otherwise neutral space. (Hint: Black paint is a great way to add more architectural personality to your home.)

Now, I have lived with mostly white or pale walls with color in the accessories for years and years now. It's always been the backdrop I've felt most comfortable with. I love the idea of color in fabrics and accessories bringing life and energy to my neutral backdrops. That being said, in most of my houses I've had at least one room with colored walls. Even if the color is subdued, a color other than white often gives rooms without a lot of natural light a little more warmth.

Whether you're painting exteriors or interiors, ask yourself this one question before you get started selecting your home's palette: What place would you love to go for a getaway? Imagine the place in your mind. Look up images online. And use the colors you see as your inspiration.

All of the colors in your home don't have to match exactly. In fact, a mix of colors can be more interesting. Choose various shades and tones of complementary colors so the entire house feels more cohesive. (Paint stores make this easy for you by grouping colors that go together into their chip samples and design books.) For interiors, add white to a darker paint color used in one room to create a new complementary color for an adjoining room. Mix the exact same brand and sheen of paint to ensure that the paint goes on smoothly and evenly when mixed together.

When painting your exterior, use the rule of three: Choose three colors (siding, door, and trim), and then repeat variations of those colors in accessories (doormat, porch furniture, and planters). You can add coordinating pops of color with flowers, seasonal décor, and other small touches.

In a house with mostly neutral walls, we opted to paint my office navy blue. I wanted to create a beautiful place to be surrounded by life and color, but also a place I could retreat to when I need to recharge. Benjamin Moore Hale Navy paint accomplished those goals.

Surprisingly, paint colors generally should be chosen *last* when you're decorating so they can complement the design of your home. Look around at the things you love. Are you drawn to warmer or cooler tones? Warm tones can feel cozy and welcoming. Cool tones are refreshing and serene. After you know your preferences, collect some swatches in color families that most appeal to you. Then bring them home and play with them. Tape them to the walls and look at them as the light changes throughout the day. See how they go with your fabrics and pillows and floorings and furnishings. Then pick your favorites and purchase small paint samples. Try them out on your walls, see which ones speak to you after a few days, and then choose your winner and begin to complete your home transformation with color.

56

Can I Usher in Color Gently?

I've been playing it safe with white in my home. And while I still love neutrals,
I want to add some color to my decorating. What is the best way to try out some new
shades but not make a commitment to a whole bunch of color?

Carol L.

KariAnne says...

I can identify. There are days when I can't decide if I like color. I know I love neutrals, but color? I'm still a little shaky on that front. I'm just not sure I want to be in a committed relationship with color. It's too much pressure. I want to date color and hang out and maybe watch a movie with popcorn and then wrap myself in neutrals and go out on the town. It's the age-old struggle. I think I might like color. I think I might like pattern. But not too much. And not all the time. So I've perfected the art of adding color to my home without commitment. Here are a few suggestions for you to try in your home.

FLOWERS

One of the simplest ways to open the color door and make your day a little brighter is to add a pop of color to your home with flowers. Don't overthink it. Don't worry if the arrangement isn't perfect. Flowers are an easy and inexpensive way to add color in your home without a commitment. You can buy a bouquet at the grocery store for less than five dollars.

Quick tip: Stretch your flowers even further and fill multiple vases with one arrangement by adding greenery from your yard.

RUGS

Rugs are great way to add temporary color to your room because they can easily be rolled up and stored away when seasons change or when you want to rework the color scheme in a room. Using rugs in the fall and winter helps brighten a home and bring in a cozy feel. When spring and summer arrive and knock at the door? Let your floors shine and send that rug on vacation for a while.

PILLOWS

Pillows are a great way to go big with color. You can have a whole lot of pattern and color going on in one little 18" x 18" square, but it's not too overwhelming because it's such a small commitment. In fact, the size of your commitment can depend on the size of your pillow—and the number of pillows you have on display. Pillows are also a great way to try out a color in a room before you change the paint on the wall.

PAINTED FURNITURE

This commitment is a step up from the pillow stage. It introduces a little more color and is a little more permanent, but it's a great place to start. Repainting a piece of furniture is so much easier than repainting a wall.

Quick tip: If you're thinking about getting rid of a piece of furniture, try painting it first. You might just find yourself in love.

PAINTED WALLS

This is the final step to color commitment, but don't worry. You don't have to paint every wall in your home or even every wall in a room. Instead? What about painting one wall or even a part of a wall above or below a chair rail? In my office I painted a raised panel wall a gorgeous coral color. It made the room pop without needing to use a lot of color in the rest of the space.

57

Any Encouragement for a Color Coward?

I feel that I've been stuck with neutrals for too long and would really like some color.
How do I overcome my fear of using color in decorating?

Kay W.

Melissa says...

One of my great pleasures is spicing up a generally neutral color scheme with unexpected colors and accessories. You will discover a lot of freedom when you embrace an ever-evolving style. If a room or an area seems bland or lifeless, often the solution is to add a more dramatic pop of color. When this easy fix is on your radar, you'll soon notice how a color or a bright accessory speaks to you or grabs your attention. Adding a cheerful dose of color to a neutral scheme can be cheap therapy!

Here are some simple ways to bring happy hues into your home:

- Brighten up a neutral kitchen with cute new hand towels, pretty spatulas or mixing spoons, colorful bowls and mugs in charming patterns, and seasonal accessories. This makes it easy to change out your look and keep the area looking fresh and updated.

- If you're hesitant to paint your walls anything but a neutral, add some color to the furniture. Changing one feature of a furniture piece can give a room a whole new look. Paint a table or a chair the color you've always wanted to try. Add that rug you've always loved but thought might be a little too daring for your comfort zone. You can also embellish walls, bookcases, or cabinets with heavy-duty wrapping paper or wallpaper. I once tacked up some pretty colored maps to a wall in a small hallway. They added color and personality without a permanent commitment. Look for colors and designs you love and make them part of what you have.

- Delight in the discovery of new colors. When browsing at antique or home furnishing stores, take pictures of any appealing tones or color combinations. Pin your favorite looks. Take note of what colors you find yourself returning to again and again and again.

- Don't miss the details. You can keep your neutral walls and furnishings if those are what appeal to you and make you feel at home. It's easy to add color to your surroundings in other ways—a vase of freshly picked wildflowers, a sunny yellow throw, pops of pink and orange in your pillows, colored baskets and containers, even patterned picture frames and interesting vases. If something speaks to you, snatch it up and display it. Watch the cheer of color spread from room to room.

- Don't rule out the addition of color to restful areas like a bedroom or bathroom. You might be tempted to keep these spaces neutral, but they can also benefit from a soft or even a deep moody tone on the walls. To update your color palette without too much commitment, add a new colorful bath rug, brightly patterned pillow shams, and other welcoming accessories. You don't have to add too many hues—especially if space is limited—but a little colorful cheer will go a long way.

- If you're unsure about which tones to introduce into your home, select a color or two from a favorite print or painting you have on the wall or plan to put up as a signature piece or focal point. This simple method will provide you with a cohesive color palette for a room, an area, or your entire interior.

I'm Inspired for a Color Scheme. Now What?

I have a painting and some accessories (like pillows) that I love. Can I base the paint color for a room around these items? And how does that work?

Katherine C.

KariAnne says...

So many times we think we need to tackle a big project first—like the walls—before we can finish the rest of the design. But if you already have colors and patterns in place that you love, why reinvent the color wheel? Instead, allow your accessories to dictate the color of your paint. Sometimes choosing a wall color after you've already chosen your accessories can really tie your decorating scheme together.

When choosing a paint color, you also want to take your floor color into account. Next to your walls, your floors are the largest surface area in your space. Look at the undertones of your linoleum or tile or carpet. Even hardwood floors have their own hues—warm or cool. If you aren't using an area rug in the space, the floor plays an even bigger part in your color decisions.

Let your furniture do the talking. Listen to your sofa or your rug or your curtains. They know what's up. Select a color you like from the pattern on a favorite statement piece in your space. The paint color doesn't have to be an exact match—just make sure to stay in the same color family with a similar hue. Typically, the room color is a

bit lighter than the color of your statement piece. Determine if your furniture and accessories set either a warm or cool tone for the room and follow their lead. Working with accessories and furniture you already have in the space makes the whole paint-choosing process so much easier and less expensive.

Last, factor in the size and shape of your room and the amount of light it receives throughout the day. In a large room with lots of light, use a more saturated color. Use color to layer a little more cozy into a room as well. A small room works well when painted with a more saturated color. If it doesn't receive a lot of natural light, or has a lot of corners and shadows, aim for a lighter tone.

Quick tip: You don't necessarily have to paint it white. Light neutrals also make a space appear larger. Lighter and brighter colors make a room feel more comfortable and functional.

Will Paint Pull Together a Look?

I'm ready to get going on the painting part of decorating my home.
What are some of your tried-and-true tips for pulling everything together with paint?

Karen J.

Melissa says...

There's no backdrop in your home bigger or more important than the walls, and the color you choose will make a huge impact on the visual flow and mood of each room—and of your entire home. But there's no need to stress out about painting! With a little know-how, you can create a look you love that's perfect for your home and your own personal style.

1 **Find inspiration everywhere for your colors.** Look around at nature, books, rugs, paintings, fabrics, accessories, landscape tones—everywhere and anywhere. You can even think of your favorite decorating shops and websites. What is the general mood you want your home to reflect, and how can you capture this mood through color?

2 **Play it safe—and then branch out from there.** If you're overwhelmed with paint choices (a common dilemma), start with a pleasing neutral wall color throughout your home. Your home will feel fresh and clean. You can always add a new color to a space in the future when you feel inspired.

3 **There's nothing wrong with neutrals.** If you have good, natural light, all-white walls can work as the perfect backdrop. If you're lacking natural light, though, add some color. A soft taupe or other neutral with color can go a long way in warming up a room. And allow your bright and cheerful accessories to warm it up even more!

4 **Soften any harsh lines with your paint scheme.** If your home has awkward angles, one tone on the walls, ceiling, and even trim can reduce the sharp lines and help the space flow better.

5 **If you want to take a fun risk, paint stripes or another pattern.** Stripes on just one wall can bring a room visual depth and space—and add a unique, personalized flair. (Hint: Research some examples before you attempt this trick. Stripes can make a great statement. You just need the right style in the right space.)

6 **Test your choices.** Before you spring for a gallon of the color you're convinced you *must* have, paint a large sample section of that color on several walls and observe it for a few days. Look at it as the light in the room changes throughout the day. Does it look like you imagined it would? Does it seem too dark or too light? Too warm

or too cold? Make adjustments until you're satisfied, and only *then* buy that gallon and begin your transformation.

7. **Have some fun!** Paint comes in so many options. Chalkboard or dry-erase paint are well suited for an office space, kids' rooms, the pantry (which helps with your grocery lists), or on an interior door. Research various finishes to get the correct type of paint for the correct room and surface.

Don't be afraid to ask questions at your favorite paint store. They're there to help you get the look you love!

60

Sign Me Up for Paint Terminology 101.

Help! I'm stuck in the paint store. I've done a good job choosing the colors I like and have decided on a palette. But now I'm confused about the different terms and finishes. What's the difference between saturation and sheen? And can I use the same paint in the kitchen and the bedroom?

Maria C.

KariAnne says...

Paint has a language all its own. It's like learning an entirely different vocabulary. Start with a few basic terms and build upon those to learn how to speak "paint." Here's a quick primer (no pun intended) on what you need to know.

First, let's start with the basic definitions:

Dry to recoat: The stage of drying when the next coat can be applied

Faux bois: A paint treatment that mimics the look of wood grain

Glaze: A medium mixed paint used to create faux finishes

Hue: A color or shade

Primer: A product applied as a first layer to help prepare the surface for painting

Saturation: The intensity of the color; the visual strength of a surface color

Sheen: A soft luster on the surface

Trompe l'oeil: Painting designed to recreate the look of a three-dimensional object

Next, let's take a closer look at different definitions of paint sheens. Here is some basic information to help you chose your paint for your next project.

Flat: This paint sheen lacks any finish or shine. Paint can almost appear to be chalky. Many times flat paint is used to absorb light.

Eggshell: This paint sheen has slightly more finish than flat but less than satin. It's a great choice to hide imperfections on the wall.

Satin: An excellent choice for most walls, it has a soft, warm luster that slightly reflects light but doesn't have too much of a shine.

Semigloss: Used for trim or doors, this paint provides a glossy sheen without too much shine.

Gloss: This paint sheen has the highest level of shine and is the most durable. It's an ideal choice for kitchens, bathrooms, and other high traffic areas, as it's very easy to wipe clean.

I send you off toward your personal painting success story with these two additional tips:

1. **Make sure you have the right tools.** Take inventory of what you need before heading out to the paint store. The most overlooked tool? A paint roller extension. You'll need one when you paint the ceiling.

2. **Calculate how much paint you'll need.** Typically, a can of paint will cover 400 square feet. Most rooms require two cans of paint to cover the entire space adequately.

You are now fluent in paint. Isn't it a colorful language?

61

Will You Shed Light on Selecting Paint Colors?

I'm having a challenging time picking paint colors for my home. The color looks so different depending on the room it's in—and depending on the time of day and how much light is in the room. What are some of your tips for choosing paint colors that work?

Mandy T.

KariAnne says...

Picking a paint color can seem like an overwhelming process. I get it. Here's the thing: It doesn't have to be. You've got this. Truly. You *can* choose a paint color you will love. You *can* get it right the very first time. And you *can* confidently stride into the paint store, armed with knowledge and wisdom. You just need to keep a few key things in mind:

- **Start your paint color journey with the darkest color at the bottom of the paint strip.** Begin by selecting two (or three) paint chip sample strips in the color you like. Although the colors may look exactly alike, they're not. Each strip is tinted in a slightly different direction. A khaki could have a pink base or a blue base. A gold can have a green base or a brown base. To see the true color tint, look at the darkest color on the strip. It has the most color saturation, and it will help you narrow down your choices.

- **A paint color can look different in your home.** It depends on your surface. If you are painting a ceiling any color other than white, go at least one shade lighter

than your walls. Color always appears darker on a ceiling. For a floor, always go one or two shades lighter. The color on the floor appears darker than on the wall. When you're looking at a paint chip in the store, hold it next to something white to see its true color—holding it next to another color can throw off how it really looks.

- **Keep saturation in mind.** Please, please remember this when you're standing in front of that paint display. Once you decide on the color you want—that perfect off-white or warm gray or breathtaking blue—go one shade darker. I know it might seem counterintuitive, but trust me on this. Natural light and tons of "stuff" tend to wash out your first color choice. Paint typically looks a little lighter when you actually get it home and on your walls. You—and your room—will be happier with a little saturation.

- **Rely on samples.** For under seven dollars, you can purchase a paint sample. Please do not let seven dollars come between you and the perfect paint color. Paint that sample on a piece of poster board and move it to different parts of the room. Look at it in the morning and at night. Examine it from every angle and in every light before you make your decision.

When you go to the paint store and choose your paint color, the process begins with a tinted base that is mixed with different colors. But did you know that no one can of paint is exactly the same as another? They're usually so close that maybe you won't see the difference—but don't take the chance. Buy a five-gallon bucket and mix your cans together before you paint. Seriously. You don't want a two-tone painted room.

If you follow these tips, you can choose your paint color with confidence.

62

So. Many. Colors. How Do I Choose?

I'm completely overwhelmed by the process of choosing the correct color and finish for interior paint. I've tried paint swatches on the walls but am still not happy with my results. How do I choose the best shades?

Scarlette C.

Melissa says...

The process of picking a paint color can be exhilarating—at first. You stand in the paint store, inspired by all the options and combinations. You thrill at the thousands of paint swatches lined up in neat little rows. But a few minutes later you find yourself feeling paralyzed and confused. Which one is right for your space? Will the color you love in the store look all wrong when you get it on the walls at home? Where should you even begin?

I love paint, and I've experienced a lot of trial and error. Here are six tips I've relied on for deciding on a color palette that's a perfect fit and not a disappointment:

1 Choose your paint color last. When you first move into a new home or remodel or reorganize your current home, it's nice if you can paint the walls first to give yourself a clean slate. But sometimes when you're decorating a room, choosing the paint color first can be a mistake. Paint colors should complement—not determine—your decorating choices. Putting the wrong color on your walls can throw off your entire decorating scheme.

2 Try recommended paint palettes if you're overwhelmed by your choices. If you have no idea which shade of white to pick from the sea of thousands or what colors might go together for your home, simplify your options. Start with the paint manufacturer color cards, and then branch out from there. You can even match your palette to a favorite piece: a fabulous throw or a pretty patterned pillow. For the record, my favorite white is Benjamin Moore Simply White.

3 Take your time selecting colors to avoid impulsive, disappointing decisions. Unless you have a keen eye for color, you'll need to give yourself time to live with a color in all kinds of light before you can be certain you'll love it long term. Gray walls may seem like a perfect choice one day, but the next day, when the lighting changes, you realize they've turned an unfortunate shade of blue. Don't choose a color because it's a designer's favorite or because it's lovely in your friend's bedroom. It might not work in your home. So take time to ensure your color choice is the shade you expect and one that becomes *your* favorite.

4 White walls won't necessarily make a room feel bigger or brighter without natural light. Even if it looks striking in an inspiration photo, the impact of white walls depends on the elements in a room. If the room lacks natural light from windows and doors or is small, white could just make it feel flat and lifeless. The best way to lighten a room and make it feel more spacious and open is to paint the walls a soft, neutral color or even go bold and select a darker color for a striking and cozier vibe. Use lighting, mirrors, and white furniture to further open up the space.

5 The best paint sheen for main living areas is satin or eggshell. Flat paint can be very pretty when it's newly painted, but I find it to be more difficult to keep fresh and clean. For trim work, bathrooms, or kitchen cabinets, I recommend a high-quality satin or semigloss.

6 The ceiling is "the fifth wall" in a room. Don't overlook it when it comes time to paint! Flat white is usually a safe choice, but some rooms will feel cozier with colored ceilings.

I used SW Mindful Gray on my kitchen island. It was the perfect neutral to balance the cool tones of the white surfaces and the warm tones of wood floor while adding dimension to the space.

How Do I Choose from the Array of Grays?

How do you choose the right tone of gray? I'm finding that different grays have different undertones—yellow, green, brown, etc. And some grays are cool, while others are warm. How do you decide on the one gray that complements your room?

Lisa C.

KariAnne says...

You've finally found your paint color. You've eliminated all the whites, blues, greens, and yellows. You're going to keep it simple and paint a room—or even a piece of furniture—a nice, simple, subtle shade of gray. How hard can it be? And then you discover there isn't just one gray that works, or even ten. Instead, there are dozens.

Truth? A gray is not always a gray. I know. It sounds weird, but it's true. Sometimes a gray looks perfect in the paint store, but when you take it home and start painting, it just doesn't look right. It's too pink. Or too green. Or too light. Or too dark. Or too warm. Or too cool.

No worries. We've got this. I'm best friends with gray, and I've discovered a few gray superstars along the way. I want to introduce you to some of my favorites by Sherwin-Williams. Here are four of my favorite gray paint colors in the universe. They are tried and true.

MINDFUL GRAY SW 7016

At first glance, this paint chip might look a little khaki, but it's not. In fact, it's the perfect not-too-green, not-too-pink gray. Not too warm or too cool. It's the Switzerland of all grays—right in the middle. And perfect every time.

JOGGING PATH SW 7638

Add a hint more of khaki to Mindful Gray, and you have Jogging Path. Imagine the color of stones you find down by the lake. It's the perfect base coat for any furniture project and looks amazing paired with navy and white. (Hint: When used in a room with white moldings, it looks darker than the paint chip.)

FAWN BRINDLE SW 7640

This is the darkest of my favorite grays. I love it as an accent color to imitate the look of weathered wood. For a perfect gray/khaki combo, layer Fawn Brindle SW 7640 with Rice Grain SW 6155.

SEDATE GRAY SW 6169

This is my go-to gray for stripes. This almond gray looks fresh and current and is wonderful when painted on a white background. Showing a hint of khaki, it can be the ideal light gray to use on a wall that gets a lot of sunlight. It's more of a beige, but looks grayer when paired with white. If you're not convinced that gray is your thing and you like a hint of color, give Sedate Gray a try.

Will Painted Furniture Paint Me into a Corner?

I love painted furniture, but I'm a little scared about how to start. Part of me wants to paint some of my existing wood furniture (such as mahogany pieces), but part of me is unsure. Can you give me some help?

Sue A.

Melissa says...

I completely understand! But life is too short to live in fear. I am not skilled at painting furniture, but when a particular piece begs for a new look, I attempt it anyway. If I take the time to do it right, I'm quite happy with the results. I encourage you to give it a try. Here are a few simple instructions.

1. **Don't skip any steps.**

2. **Give the piece a good sanding.** Remove any residue that might interfere with your paint job.

3. **Prime it.** Then sand it again to eliminate any bumps caused by drips.

4. **Paint it carefully.** Make sure you add enough coats so it shines. Patience and effort will get you there.

5. **Protect it.** Use a good finish to prevent chipping and peeling.

6. **Finally, don't worry!** Be brave, do what you love, and enjoy the results.

Now, let me inspire and encourage you. Wood furniture lovers might become upset with you for painting a piece, but it's okay. I love wood furniture and have several gorgeous pieces in my home, but I don't like *too much* or *too many kinds* in one space. And if a piece of furniture is in need of a makeover, I'm willing to pick up a paintbrush in order to fall in love with it all over again.

Case in point is an adorable little coffee table I'd had for a long time. I'd bought it years ago right off the truck of an antique dealer during our neighborhood's annual garage sale. It was perfect in one of my homes, but when I moved to a larger home, it was too tiny for my rooms. So it hung out in my garage, just waiting to be loved again.

When I rediscovered it, I knew I wanted to use it. Yet its worn wood top and dark orange wood finish didn't appeal to me any longer. What to do? I didn't just paint over the wood—I painted it BRIGHT BLUE. Not a respectable color such as white or gray or black or even teal. My husband almost had a heart attack, but I loved it and he actually did too.

That story is my permission to you to become a decorating rebel. If you have a piece of furniture you love the look of but the wood finish makes you cringe, perhaps it's time to break out the paint and paintbrush.

I painted this pine table just before Thanksgiving dinner one year. Sometimes the pressure of guests on their way inspires me to take swift action on a project. If you don't like a wood piece as it is, why hesitate to paint it? Chances are you'll like it far more than you did previously.

65

Are Kids and Neutrals Allowed to Coexist?

My favorite palette is a neutral palette, but I don't think that light colors are practical in my house with active children around. And I'm not a big fan of dark colors. Is there any way to get the look I love without having stains everywhere?

Wanda G.

KariAnne says...

One of the questions I get asked most often when I speak at an event is: "Do you really like all the neutral colors in the house?" And then the question asker always follows up with: "Do children really live in a house with all that white furniture?" I smile and nod and giggle to myself and say yes. Yes, I'm all about neutrals. And yes, children—and a dog or two—really do live in a house with white furniture.

We live in a house with four children, three cats, and three dogs. Seriously. *My secret?* It's a microfiber cloth you use to scrub down upholstery with water. Just scrub the fabric a little with the cloth, and the dirt usually dissolves. Kind of like a magic eraser for furniture. You can keep your spaces relatively stain-free. All you need are the right cleaning tools and a little patience with your neutral furniture—and keep strawberry soda in the kitchen. Now that we know the secret formula for keeping neutral upholstery clean, here are a few tips on adding neutrals to your décor:

- **All neutrals were not created equal.** Did you know there are 5,026 shades of white? Okay—maybe it's 5,025. I might be exaggerating a little, but all you have to do is look around you. Some whites are warm.

Some are cool. Some whites have a background of pink or yellow or gray or blue. Put several white items next to one another, and you can spot the difference. The same thing goes for other neutrals, such as gray and khaki and gold. They are all considered neutrals, but each color has so many different shades and hues. Neutrals are anything but boring.

- **Choose your paint color wisely.** Select various shades of a neutral color you are drawn to and then try them out in your home. Next, actually paint swatches on your wall. Some of my favorite neutral paint shades are from Sherwin-Williams and include Mindful Gray SW 7016, Dorian Gray SW 7017, Ivoire SW 6127, Stamped Concrete SW 7655, and Repose Gray SW 7015 (a soft, cool gray that's perfect for rooms with a lot of natural light).

- **Texture makes all the difference.** The key to making your neutral look come alive? Texture. Texture layered over texture with a little more texture on top. Think textiles and patterns and patina and fabric—just like the different textures found in wicker baskets; rustic wooden tabletops; a crinkly weathered map;

soft, raised fabric; and the aged crackle of an antique mirror. When you combine all these textures artfully together, they become the "color" in your room.

- A little greenery helps balance all that neutral. Greenery works well to enhance the brightness and lightness of neutrals. Place a galvanized bucket full of

ivy on your coffee table, tuck a pot of greenery under a cloche, or add a topiary to your kitchen sink. There's just something about a little pop of fresh greenery that makes all your neutrals sing.

66

Can Different Colors + Patterns = Cohesive?

How do you coordinate different colors and patterns in rugs, drapes, and upholstery? When does it all not go well together?

Patricia V.

Melissa says...

It might initially make you nervous to experiment with colors and patterns, but I guarantee that great joy is ahead when you begin mixing things up to give a room a special warmth and unique personality. I'll be the first to admit that mixing shades and designs may take some practice and maybe even a dose of courage! But oh, is it worth it. And personally, I'm energized when I switch from cautious to creative. I know you'll find that to be true as well.

It's such a gift to have a space where you can create a look you love. If you keep a few basic tips in mind, you'll be well on your way to a successful mix-and-match look.

1 **Be patient working with what you have.** It's easy to create a workable mix in a room when you buy everything new and choose from ready-made collections. But that can be expensive—and not very original anyway. The challenge comes when you bring in your grandma's colorful Persian rug and your mother-in-law's favorite antique sofa with your collection of flea market throw pillows. That's going to take a lot more time and a lot more patience. The upside? Your house is going to look amazing and one of a kind!

2 **Be resourceful.** Maybe you have a vision in mind for what you want your space to be like, but the items you want to work with don't seem to play nicely together. You can pare down the patterns or colors in the room until you're happy with the result (perhaps you could put the rug in another room if it's fighting with the sofa), or you can tone down the impact by bringing in more solids and neutrals or by varying the scale of your patterns. For instance, if you have too many large patterns screaming for attention, add in a smaller-scale pattern to create a more pleasing mix.

3 **Take some risks.** We all need to develop our eye for mixing patterns so eventually we won't have to overthink things. The more you experiment, the sooner you'll get to the point where you can just *know* if the patterns play nicely together and the room works or not. You develop that eye through a lot of trial and error and a willingness to attempt to put things together in a way you might not normally try.

4 **Start small.** If you're starting fresh with pattern mixing, begin with a solid white as a foundation and then add in one basic color in both a large-scale and

a small-scale pattern. You can't go wrong with this combo, but I encourage you to take it a step further. Mix in a few more colors and several scales of patterns. Try stripes with a large scale geometric. Add in a floral. See what works for you.

5   **Visualize.** Don't be afraid to bring a variety of unexpected patterns together. You don't have to make everything match or look perfect—just have things look appealing together.

6   **Stash some samples.** You can carry around little fabric swatches or paint chips, and you can also store the images on your phone. Take pictures of your rooms and close-ups of your rugs, pillows, and curtains. That way you can always have your decorating scheme at the ready when you happen upon a great deal or what looks to be the perfect piece. If you scroll through your photos and check out what you already have to go with the new pattern, you can save yourself the hassle of making a mistake or purchasing something you already own.

67

Can I Express Creativity and Avoid Clash?

With so many gorgeous prints and patterns and colors to choose from, how do I even begin? I'm not sure how to coordinate my decorating scheme. I want to be creative, but I don't want everything to clash.

Barbara W.

KariAnne says...

I get it. I understand. But choosing a fabric for your home is a lot like planning a first-day-of-school outfit in high school—all you need is a really good pair of shoes. Start with your foundation and build your design around that. For example, the next time you walk into a fabric store, trust your intuition. Walk the aisles slowly and carefully, looking at each of the bolts of fabric to find two or three extraordinary fabrics that take your breath away. Then ask for samples. Take them home and live with them. If you find you can't live without a certain fabric, you know you've found your foundation fabric. Use that pattern to create the rest of your design. Here are a few tips for figuring out which patterns will work in your space:

1 **Embrace the rule of threes.** It's a design truth: everything looks better together when they're grouped in arrangements of odd numbers. That same truth applies to fabrics as well. Start with three patterns and then add more if needed.

2 **Pay attention to scale.** Start with your largest-scale pattern and use it as your guide. This should be the pattern we talked about above—one that inspires you to build the whole room around it. This fabric sets the tone for the entire space. After you've settled on your primary pattern, choose another pattern that's half the scale of that one and then finish your pattern selection with an even smaller pattern design.

3 **Follow the 60/30/10 formula.** Use the pattern you like best in 60 percent of your decorating choices. Use a smaller coordinating pattern in 30 percent of your décor, and then layer in the remaining pattern 10 percent of the time.

4 **Remember the solids.** When deciding on patterns, it's easy to forget about choosing a solid. Solid fabrics are so important. They're the supporting cast. Never underestimate the function of an amazing solid-colored fabric.

Quick design tip: Solids don't have to be boring. Just look how beautiful linen and velvet are.

5 Repeat and balance. All the fabrics you choose don't necessarily have to be different patterns. For example, two different types of florals can work well together in a room. Or two polka dots. Or two stripes or geometric patterns. Just vary the size and scale of each design to make it work—like pairing a larger floral with a smaller one.

6 Strategically place patterns. If all your patterns hang out together on one side of the room, they tend to make your space feel lopsided. Distribute pattern evenly throughout the room to create a cohesive look.

7 Take another look. Before selecting a large-scale pattern for your home, step back several feet and observe it from a distance. This perspective gives you a better idea of how the pattern will look in the room. It can be hard to determine how larger patterns will fit in a space from looking at just a small swatch.

8 Audition it. Sometimes it's a good idea to try out a pattern before you choose it for something big, such as curtains or even a sofa or chair. Date it on a pillow for a few weeks before you make a lasting commitment.

9 Make room for white space. Patterns are gorgeous and amazing, but everyone needs a little break now and then. Patterns should be used as an accent to bring life and color to a room, not to fill and overpower it.

68

How Do I Decorate with Fabrics?

I love to buy items and reupholster or refinish them. My biggest hurdle is selecting fabrics. Can you give me some pointers on decorating with fabrics—patterns, colors, styles, etc.?

Robin Y.

Melissa says...

Pulling together fabrics can really inspire the feel of a house. I find the easiest way to begin is with a statement fabric—whatever you want to be the boldest pattern in the room. Then you can more easily begin to play around with additional patterns and colors until you come up with a combination that inspires you.

If you want to have fun with a pattern mix, look for a small print to complement your bold pattern and add some stripes, checks, polka dots, light backgrounds, colored backgrounds, solids—whatever catches your eye. Pin swatches on an inspiration board with a few paint samples. Then make a list of the ways you could use your favorite fabrics around your home.

Now comes the fun part—choosing decorating fabrics for various rooms. We can bring the beauty and diversity of fabrics into our spaces in so many ways.

- Drape fabric over a lackluster chair as a slipcover. Consider drapes, sheets, and bolts of fabric as potential material for this furniture refresh.

- Cover well-worn pillows with fabric to give them an instant update. Vary the scale of the patterns so the overall effect in the room is pleasing. You can even change out the fabrics by season.

- When determining fabric for decorative pillows, you can use a 2-2-1 formula. Two matching, equally sized and shaped pillows on either end of a sofa; two smaller, like-sized pillows in a different fabric next to them; and one smaller accent pillow in the middle. Here are two possible fabric combinations:

  1. Two matching polka dot outer pillows, two matching floral inner pillows, one solid middle pillow

  2. Two matching solid outer pillows, two matching striped or plaid inner pillows, one floral middle pillow

- To prevent color and pattern overload, choose a couple of colors (for instance, shades of blue and white) and stick to that color scheme as you add fabrics. Once you've mastered the basics, mix in an additional color or two to provide pop.

- Two similar fabrics will look best together when they're connected by a common color.

A pinstripe fabric is a classic choice for an upholstered sofa, bench, or settee. We finished the look with two boldly patterned pillows and a textured neutral pillow.

- You can combine three or more fabrics in a room, but be sure to start simply. Choose a large-scale pattern and a small-scale pattern in the same color family. Then mix in some solids and a few more patterns that seem to go with the others.

- Generally, it's safer to mix fabric patterns in similar styles (traditional with traditional or contemporary with contemporary). Fabric manufacturers make it easy these days by releasing collections. The patterns and colors are varied, but all of the fabrics in the collection should work well together.

Take time to enjoy this process. Give yourself permission to experiment, mix things up, and display the colors and patterns you love.

Organization

While most of us can agree that decorating is fun, albeit not always easy, organization is the category where some of us part ways. There are people who are born organizers, and there are people for whom chaos is a constant and organization seems an impossible dream. With the right tips and tools, though, you can have a home with terrific style *and* organization. It just takes a few tools, a little forethought, and a willingness to work at it.

Need a little more inspiration to get organized? You can combine organizing with decorating! There's no need to fill your home with dull containers or unsightly plastic bins and boxes. Some of the best clutter catchalls double as simply stunning decorating pieces. And there's also no need to spend a ton of money. You'd be surprised at the organizing tools that already inhabit your home. Get ready to clear out some space and take some steps toward order *and* beauty in the home. We promise it will be relatively painless—even if you're not a born organizer!

69

How Do I Downsize My Décor?

Big-time decorating dilemma here! I've collected so many things, and I feel compelled to display them all. The result? My rooms are on major overload! Any helpful hints for paring things down?

Sue S.

KariAnne says...

Accessories are my best friends too. And really, they're good friends to have. They can bring back delightful memories or simply make you smile. And there's nothing an accessory can't do. Truly, they're the superheroes of the decorating world. Sometimes small but always mighty, the perfect accessory gives the room just the right touch. It can leap bookcases in a single bound. It can save a hutch that's about to make a wrong turn. It can rescue a wall that's lost its way and save a kitchen island that's far from home.

Do you get my point? I. Love. Accessories. And you can find them anywhere. They're easily acquired at yard sales and in thrift stores and discovered in your grandmother's attic. You can tweak them and turn them and twist them this way and that. You can pair them with friends or allow them to make a statement all on their own.

An accessory allows you to showcase your personality and your heart. That one-of-a-kind overstuffed ottoman with swimming mermaids you found at an auction? If it screams *you*, by all means, rock it in your home! It's your house and your space, and you have all the permission in the world to decorate it with the things you love.

As you're assessing your accessories and trying to decide if you're perhaps a little on overload, keep switching things in and out until you've hit on what seems to be a comfortable balance. And remember, you don't have to display every item during every season. Most of us have Christmas boxes we haul out of storage shortly after Thanksgiving. But create boxes of decorations for the other seasons as well. Every season is fair game for doing up your décor! Have a spring box, a summer box, an autumn box, and a winter box. This also helps you pare down your decorations and makes it easier to put things away at the end of a season. When you know you'll be able to bring a favorite item out again in a few months, it won't be a big deal to store it away temporarily.

I'll send you off here with a few fun guidelines for awesome accessorizing:

- Always remember that a frame (or a really pretty glass cloche) makes everything seem more important. If you have something you want to showcase—such as a playbill or a wedding invitation or the race number from a run you completed—frame it, and it immediately becomes art.

- If one of something is good, three or more of that same thing can be amazing. Even the simplest of objects becomes so much more when the rest of its family shows up for the reunion.

- Finally, have fun! I once hung some tiny chairs on a wall, and they were the talk of the county. Don't take your accessories too seriously. Trust me—your home will thank you.

70

Can Style Success Happen in This Mess?

I love looking through decorating magazines and blogs and dreaming about how I would like my home to look. But what do I do with our everyday life stuff? My husband and I both work from home, and parts of our house look as if a tornado just hit. What can I do?

Kathleen B.

Melissa says...

When you're living life *and* working from home, it can be easy for the everydayness of life (and the clutter!) to elevate your stress levels. What are the everyday things that distract from your sense of style and peace? Observe your home for a week. What are the messes that pile up? What clutter causes you frustration? What are the items you don't like to see lying around the house? What causes the tornado?

My husband likes to use our small galley kitchen as his office. Honestly, I've never seen so many sticky notes on a counter! (He would be the first to admit that his system isn't ideal.) While it's tempting to focus on who is responsible for pileups or try to change someone else's habits, I find that approach hasn't been nearly as effective for me as coming up with creative solutions for housekeeping that will work for everyone.

My approach to these every day dilemmas is three-fold:

1 **Color coordinate.** It might seem a little obsessive, but I find it helps to streamline the stuff I keep out as much as possible and then try to color coordinate the necessary tools and accessories of daily life (I do this over time as I'm able to!). Why shouldn't the laundry baskets on the floor blend in with your style? A rattan laundry basket full of white towels sitting out is less distracting to me than my old lime green plastic one that was filled with a rainbow assortment of mismatched towels.

2 **Corral clutter.** Choose attractive, consistent places to store everyday items. An antique dresser can be your organizer for your office and paper supplies and technology cords. A wicker basket can hold your monthly receipts. Get creative and choose pieces that suit your home's style and, when possible, select storage solutions that serve double duty. Your file cabinet might hold your office lamp stand, for example.

If you find a surface is always covered with mail or random clutter (and who hasn't experienced that problem?), declare that surface a clutter-free zone. A closed cabinet, cork board, or lidded basket can be a less stressful place to stash the everyday stuff (even those sticky notes) that used to accumulate on the surface. (Until you have time to deal with it, of course. If a clutter holder fills up, you'll know it's past time to return everything to its proper place!)

3   **Develop sanity systems.** This is a biggie when it comes to sanity, productivity, and a tidy, attractive home. Systems are everything. Go back to your list of offending stuff. What new systems could you establish to keep the daily tornado from turning a peaceful oasis into a workday disaster zone?

- Make it a daily habit to make the beds and wipe out the sinks before you start work so you have less mess to look at.

- Perhaps start a ten-minute lunchtime tidy to keep the chaos from getting out of hand.

- Delegate essential chores for the hour before dinner so everyone can enjoy a more restful evening at home.

- Find a household assistant to take care of simple housekeeping tasks for you. A professional might not be in the budget, but even a child or neighborhood teen could handle tasks such as unloading the dishwasher, cleaning counters, vacuuming, dusting, and folding and putting away laundry. Assign an assistant the responsibility of keeping key surfaces clear and cleaning up any mess that distracts from the beauty of a room.

BY WISDOM A HOUSE IS BUILT AND THROUGH UNDERSTANDING IT IS ESTABLISHED; THROUGH KNOWLEDGE ITS ROOMS ARE FILLED WITH RARE AND BEAUTIFUL TREASURES
PROVERBS 24:3

71

Can I Host and Have a Life?

Hospitality is important to me. I want to make my home inviting to those who enter, but how do I balance this with my busy life? I don't have time to be constantly cleaning and decorating!

Rita G.

KariAnne says...

Amen. Come and sit by me. I love having people over and entertaining and welcoming others into my home. I like having my home sparkling clean—you know, with everything dust-free and put away and shiny and tidy and in its place. It's the *getting there* that I don't like—the dusting and vacuuming and mopping and swishing and washing. If you're happy with your home when it's clean, others will feel happy and comfortable in it too. (Total grammar aside: Have you ever noticed that *vacuum* is a super hard word to spell?)

Don't have time to clean? No worries. You can take it from messy to clean in minutes with this simple checklist of ten cleaning shortcuts. (Each tip takes five minutes or less, so you can get your entire home company ready in about an hour.) My favorite tip? I spray the cleaner onto the towel and then wipe things down to make the process go a little faster.

1. **Table and chair legs.** Grab a flour sack cloth and swipe down as many chair and table legs as you can in five minutes. This is also the perfect job for all the spare socks sitting around the laundry room. Spray down the sock with a little furniture polish, wipe away the cobwebs, and watch your furniture sparkle.

2. **Refrigerator.** Wipe down as much of the fridge as you can. Open the doors. Clean the sides. Pull out the little tray where the ice maker is and discover an entire dirt colony you never knew existed and show it the door.

3. **Mirrors and faucets.** I use a flour sack rag for these items too.

4. **Extra serving platters and dishes.** Get your platters ready for last-minute guests. Gather up those dust-collecting decorator dishes and run a quick rinse cycle in your dishwasher. Place them back onto the shelf sparkling and clean. It's almost as if you just shopped your house for new party supplies.

5. **Doorknobs.** Snag your trusty flour sack cloth, spritz it with a little cleaner, and walk through your house swiping each and every doorknob. Don't limit yourself to just the handle. Be sure to clean around the edges and in the grooves and polish up all the sides where dirt tends to hide.

6. **Silverware drawer.** Sometimes I open up my drawer and shudder and shut it again. I'm not sure when and

I'm not sure why, but somewhere along the way all those spoons and forks got mixed together with extra dust and dirt. Take out the utensil holder and clean it, put the silverware back where it goes, and clean underneath the organizer too.

7   **Trash cans.** Sometimes the bottom of a trash can smells worse than a stinky sock. Take the cans outside, empty them, spray the bottoms with your favorite scented cleaner, let them soak for a few minutes, and then rinse and dry them before you put a liner back in. (Total trash can aside: Add scented liners to keep everything smelling fresh.)

8   **Ceiling fan.** I have a round tool with bristles that fits right over the blade of the fan. Start by turning your fan off and then slide the brush over each of the blades. I like to put a drop cloth below the fan to catch the dust.

9   **Sink.** Wipe down the handles, clean the gunk out of the grooves on the outside, wipe off everything with a sponge, and then give it one final swipe with a dry towel to make it shine.

10   **Sheets.** A regular sheet-changing schedule is a wonderful thing, but I tend to forget. Don't let life get in the way of your sheet changing. An easy solution is to set aside one day of the week for changing sheets and then stick to your sheet-changing schedule.

Now that your house is clean, take a moment to fluff your spaces. Add a vase of fresh flowers, plump up the pillows, spray some scented room freshener, and your home is ready for company.

72

Which Changes Will Maximize a Small Entry?

I have hardly any space in the entryway of my 400-year-old English home. What is the best, most functional, and prettiest way to utilize a small entryway so that coats, shoes, and umbrellas are not all you see.

Cindy C.

Melissa says...

Welcoming others into your home can be challenging with a small entryway—or a nonexistent entry! Many older homes have limited space when you walk in the door, or you simply enter right into the living room. It's nice to provide a transition between indoor and outdoor spaces, and with a little creativity you can make this happen. The biggest challenge with a small entryway is definitely how to make it both functional and charming.

Here are some tips to help you shape a streamlined and welcoming entry:

• **Reallocate storage to an adjoining space.** If you want to keep your entry clear of belongings, designate a furniture piece or closet in another space as the place to organize items from the entryway. For instance, an antique armoire in the living room could become the place where you store coats and umbrellas.

• **Keep a small entryway tidy.** Focus on incorporating stylish storage options and organizers just for the essentials of life into the design of your entry. First remove unnecessary, excess, and out-of-season items. Scour secondhand stores for unique pieces that add form and function to your space: repurposed metal buckets and plant stands, old crates, a small table. Even corralling umbrellas in a funky stand can enhance the style of an entry, add a touch of charm, and serve a useful purpose. In a tiny entry, the only available space might be on the wall, so use it to your advantage. For convenience and style, attach some interesting hooks for your keys and most-used seasonal jackets and umbrellas. Keep shoes in a basket near the door or tucked just inside another room.

• **Think about the ambience you want to create for friends and family who walk in the door.** Focus on pretty touches that make a small entry more welcoming. Lay down a small rug to add a colorful statement at the front door. Hang a rustic lantern or a small candle holder with a battery-operated candle on a wall near the door. When guests are visiting (or just for you!), light a candle and turn on your lamps, have some music playing, and remember to keep the porch light on when it's dark.

• **Create a pretty focal point.** Set up a pretty focal point to be the highlight of a functional and hardworking entry. A small table, cabinet, or bench can house a stunning seasonal display of blossoms or a small stack of books and an attractive lamp. A bold mirror or a mini gallery wall of favorite photos can work as well. If your entry opens right into another room, make the focal point in the adjoining space as welcoming as possible.

Little touches like these go a long way toward welcoming others into your home.

73

My Junk Drawer Takes Over My Décor. Ideas?

I'd love for all my decorating and accessorizing to really shine, but I'm having trouble staying on top of things with my organizing. Do you have any tips for taming a junk drawer (or a junk shelf...or even a junk closet)?

Lanita A.

KariAnne says...

I have a cabinet in my house that attacked me last week. *Seriously.* I'm so not even kidding. Like something out of a horror movie. I opened the doors to retrieve a plastic container for leftovers, and do you know what happened? Two pitchers, four lids, a foil pan that used to cover a casserole, and 47 tiny spice jars reached out and bit me. You're not alone. This junk cabinet has friends—they're junk drawers and junk shelves and junk closets. And it might take a little effort, but trust me—they can be tamed. In the spirit of conquering our cabinets and showing the spice jars who's in charge, here are some tips for reclaiming control of your junk areas:

1. **Get ruthless.** Empty everything out of the cabinet, closet, shelf, or drawer. This project is best accomplished when you're not going to be called away five minutes later, but it's worth the time spent. You'll save so much time down the road. Now take a look at the empty space. Doesn't it look happy? Take a few more minutes to give it a good scrub-down before moving on to the next step.

2 **Sort everything into piles.** You'll have one pile for things that need to be thrown away or recycled. Another pile for items to be given away. Another for items that need to be returned to another place in the home. And your final pile will include the items that will actually live in that space.

3 **Take another look.** Scrutinize the items you're keeping. Do you really need two rolling pins or three tape dispensers or 100 hangers or 200,000 paper clips? Try to move a few more items to your discard piles.

4 **Choose containers.** First, shop your house for unused baskets, bins, crates, and other storage containers. If you need a few more, head out to your favorite thrift shop or home goods store. (But use restraint! You're trying to pare things down and get organized, remember?)

5 **Corral the paper.** Even in the digital age, paper mess tends to accumulate. You can add plastic paper sleeves to the inside of a cabinet door. This is a great place to store manuals, important school info, instruction booklets (for various appliances), your go-to handwritten recipes, and takeout menus from your favorite restaurants. Before you store paper, first figure out if the same information can be accessed online. Always be seeking out space-saving solutions.

6 **Dress it up.** Adding a pretty patterned liner to the bottom of the junk drawer or shelf helps give you the inspiration to keep it clean. After all, you want to be able to see that pretty paper! It also helps to use cute containers to separate and organize items such as paper and binder clips, pens and pencils, and thumbtacks.

74

How Can I Avoid Mid-Project Mayhem?

I love decorating and designing—but that means I'm always in the middle of one project or another. Do you have any helpful hints for getting things organized and cleaning my house—fast?

Stacey K.

KariAnne says...

We've all had *the* phone call. Or the text message. You know. The phone rings (or pings) and it's your friend who is having a jewelry party and wants to drop off a catalog for the event next week. Or your aunt who needs you to teach the Sunday school lesson and wants to leave the book at your house. Or your daughter's cheerleading coach who is dropping her off after practice and wants to talk for just a minute. When you put down the phone, you look around and realize your house may or may not closely resemble the latest episode of *Hoarders*. Yikes! What can you do before your unexpected guest pops by? Actually, all you need is 14 minutes and some of my proven tips to *faux clean* your house for company.

1. **Put on shoes.** You're going to need them to sprint (14 minutes, remember?). Kind of like getting ready for a clean-up marathon. So lace up your most comfy sneakers and line up at the start line. (If you're already wearing shoes, you're brilliant and I congratulate you.)

2. **Light some candles.** If you're wondering why, just take a sniff. What do you notice? Perhaps an aroma of needs-to-be-scooped kitty litter mixed with burnt toast with a hint of wet dog. Yes, you need the power of candles. You'll want to do this step right away so the wax has time to start melting. And once your doorbell rings and you greet the friend or aunt or cheerleading coach, they will be distracted with the gentle aroma of a salty ocean breeze or a peppermint wonderland. Seriously. Pomegranate and lemongrass make cobwebs and smelly socks fade away in the breeze. (Note: If you're sensitive to candles, you can use an essential oil diffuser. It's equally as quick and effective.)

3. **Fill your sink with soap and water.** Turn on the faucet, plug the sink, add dish soap, and fill with water. Then take all the dirty dishes and set them in that beautiful, foamy, soapy water. Next, go on a mission to gather all the cups and plates and other assorted dishes that have been visiting the other rooms of your house and add them to the sink. The soapy sink looks super cute and makes you look super productive—as if you were just about to do the dishes before you were interrupted by the doorbell.

4 Pick one room to stash everything in. Yep, it's true confession time. I really do this—and you can too. You only need to concentrate on the rooms closest to the doorbell. Choose a room out of sight as your stash room and toss everything in there. Then close the door. Do not—*I repeat*—do not open the door or reference that room in any way. Pretend it moved to Tahiti.

5 Wipe down your counters with something that smells good. I love Mrs. Meyer's products. Don't take a lot of time on this step. Your counters should already be fairly empty because the dishes are now in that soapy water. Just spray a yummy-scented cleaner and do a quick wipe-down. This creates the illusion that you recently cleaned the entire space. You can wipe down the bathroom counters as well. Now you're ready to open that door!

75

And Where Do I Put My Toaster?

I have very little space in my kitchen. How can I find storage for
all of my appliances without making the space look terribly cluttered?

Julia C.

Melissa says...

A lot happens in the kitchen: cooking, baking, preserving, conversation, gathering. Sometimes it's a puzzle to figure out how to best arrange your kitchen to be efficient as well as to allow for the most storage and counter space. Just the size of a few appliances—a microwave or toaster oven, a stand mixer, a blender, a coffee maker—can overwhelm a small area.

During one of our home remodels, I decided to temporarily store the microwave oven in the pantry. We actually rarely use a microwave, but sometimes it's nice to have one when you have a big meal or need an extra oven to heat something up or you just want a quick snack, so we set it up in the pantry during the remodel. I thought it might be inconvenient, but it turns out I preferred having the microwave in the pantry! It was fairly close and convenient, but it also freed up counter and cabinet space in the kitchen and helped us have more room to work.

Here are a few suggestions for reducing the clutter in your kitchen:

- **Group your kitchen into activity zones, and store the appropriate appliance in each zone.** I like to put all my baking supplies in one area (hello, stand mixer!) and all my cooking supplies in another (including my food processor). A cute little rolling cart makes a fun place to store coffee and tea supplies and appliances (like a Keurig). If you make a lot of smoothies, keep your blender located near the fridge so you can pull out frozen fruits and veggies, juices, and milks. (Hint: If it's easy to access the ingredients, you'll be much more likely to make healthy meals!)

- **Store large appliances you don't use every day in a separate space** (but still try to make them as accessible as possible). These items could be a Crock-Pot, a rice cooker, or a food dehydrator. Also, take a good, hard look at appliances that haven't seen the light of day in years. Do you really need that bread machine? If you haven't used it for a year or two, and it's simply taking up space and collecting dust, send it out the door to the donation bin. Sometimes simpler—a good knife and a solid cutting board—is better. When you reassess your stuff and consider removing or relocating items to create a clearer workspace, you also increase the efficiency of your storage areas.

- **See if you can move out other items to free up space for appliances.** That collection of knickknacks you have displayed on your counter? Not necessary. Plus, that new stand mixer in the gorgeous color you've always longed for is a statement piece all on its own. Store cleaning items in a decorative basket next to the sink to allow for additional space. If anything is simply decorative without being functional, it's time to clear it out. Group like items together, consolidate, and make it your goal to create as much space to work as possible.

76

Is There Storage Hope for a Small Kitchen?

My kitchen is decorated in a cute way, but it's too crowded and cluttered.
I need some help organizing it and creating effective storage solutions.
How can I make this relatively small space work for me?

Julia C.

KariAnne says...

Your kitchen is the workhorse of your home. Hundreds of meals are prepared in it each year. Countless conversations happen in that space. And sometimes the kitchen is also connected to your laundry area. But you know what they say about all work and no fun. The best way to enjoy your kitchen? Get it organized so that it works for you. If you're always scrambling to find ingredients and don't have a clue where you put your gadgets, stay tuned. Organizing is my jam, and I can help make it yours too.

1 **Make the ordinary extraordinary.** Sometimes something ordinary, such as spoons and knives and forks, can look like actual works of art when they're displayed in a unique way. I made a silverware organizer with a galvanized tin and three mason jars (for spoons, knives, and forks), and added cute chalkboard tags.

2 **Store, store away.** I organize all my paper goods—plates, plastic silverware, cups, and paper towels—in decorative storage containers, such as galvanized tins and woven baskets. Then I store them on my kitchen island. I always know where to find them, but they

look so much prettier tucked away than sitting out in the open in their original plastic packaging.

3   **Designate a place for the random.** I've selected one big basket for everything that doesn't have a place in the kitchen. On a good day, it's empty. But on a hectic day? (Okay, that covers most days!) It's filled with school papers, random earrings, even a pet toy or two. It functions as the holding place for everything that needs a home. If someone in the family is missing something, this is a good place to look.

4   **Welcome your cookbooks home.** Don't store your cookbooks on the bookshelf in the living room or even in the dining room. If you want them to get any use, store them in the kitchen—where they will be used. Plus, they add an attractive, homey touch to the room.

5   **Put things up.** Aprons, kitchen towels, pot holders, reusable grocery bags, and even knives on a magnetic strip. Hang and mount as many things as possible to free up valuable counter space.

6   **Keep your tools together.** Instead of tossing serving spoons, whisks, and ladles into a drawer (along with gadgets and other items), group them together in a cute container.

7   **Stick to one color scheme for your dishes.** White makes it simple. Even if the styles don't match, they still look nice together. If you're wanting more color, try all red or all blue. Or combine colors. Blue and white is always a classic combination. Another bonus of a simple color scheme: You're inclined to purchase fewer dishes because you can mix and match anything together.

8   **Consider open shelving.** If this idea strikes terror in your heart, hear me out. You can use baskets and bins to cut back on visual clutter. And if you stick to the all-one-color (or two colors) scheme, your open shelves can actually look like works of art.

77

Help Me Keep an Open Mind About Open Shelves.

What are some strategies for staying organized when you like the
open shelf/open closet design concepts but are naturally disorganized?
My baskets and shelves look as if mini explosions are taking place inside them!

Janet P.

Melissa says...

Open shelving design really appeals to me, and I make it work even though I'm not a naturally organized person. The open space makes everything look so much more inviting, plus it makes it easier to access items when you need them. The trick is to only display what is attractive as well as creating a system that works for you so you can easily find what you need *and* are motivated to put it back. These tips will open your mnd and shelves in no time.

- **Simplify.** If you have open shelves or any other type of visible storage that is pretty much a disaster, you need to intervene! To preserve your sanity, it's helpful to start over with a clean slate. Make a vow not to keep anything around that adds frustration to your life. Pruning the excess—even the good stuff—makes room for a more creative and fulfilling life. It also prevents feeling a little awkward when a neighbor shows up unexpectedly.

- **Start with baskets.** I love baskets. I use them all over the house, in pretty much every room. They're functional and look terrific. You can store books and magazines in baskets in the living room and family room. They corral jewelry and other items in the bedroom. And you can even use baskets in the pantry to store food! If you can't see what's in the baskets, make sure you label them so you don't forget about what's inside. I love baskets and canisters in the pantry because they cover up the packaging that may or may not be attractive. The baskets are always there looking all fancy, and it doesn't matter what the stuff looks like inside of them (as long as you can't see the contents from the room).

- **Arrange attractively.** The idea of open shelving in the kitchen might strike fear in your heart, but if you limit the shelves to hold items that are attractive, you're less likely to go wrong. If you would like open shelving for everyday dishes or pantry items in your kitchen but are afraid you'll spend the better part of each day fussing with staging your shelves, there's no need to worry. You can use your items every day, and they'll look as good next week as they do today. And you don't have to spend a fortune on fancy dishes or pantry organizers. Just remember these two guidelines:

① Group like things together (plates, bowls, and cups on their own shelf; baking supplies in attractive containers on another shelf).

② Confine the open shelving to featuring the things that complement your style. (I like all-white dishes. They are different styles, but they go together because all of them are white.)

- **Add variety.** Take the time to find cute containers—baskets, boxes, canisters, crates. You can find them inexpensively, and they do double duty as organizers and decorative items. One day of staging my open shelves gives me many years of beauty. It's worth it, and it really is that easy to have attractive shelves! I've done open cabinets or shelves in every house I've lived in—big or small—and they have never been complicated or impossible to pull off.

Seriously, you could come over and surprise me any day of the week, and my open cabinets will look just fine. And so will yours!

78

How Do I Turn My Bathroom into a Spa?

Is it really possible to have a clean and charming bathroom?
It seems I have so little space. Extra decorations make it look so messy.
How can I achieve a relaxing, spa-like feel in my bathroom and make it sparkle?

Erica L.

KariAnne says...

Sometimes organizing seems so overrated, doesn't it? Especially for a space like a bathroom. I mean, organizing your office makes sense. Or your kitchen. Or even your laundry room. A lot happens in those areas, and you need to make sure you're organized so you can be as productive as possible. But your bathroom? Actually, that makes sense too. You have a lot of supplies in your bathrooms: toiletries and towels, bath bombs and Band-Aids, soap and shaving cream, so it's helpful to keep it as neat and clean as possible. Here are ideas to create a spa feel. And when you finally have the time to take that long soak in the tub? You can just hop right in and relax.

- **Organize and decorate with your towels.** I keep a stack of new, white fluffy towels in a metal basket next to the bathtub along with the softest rug ever created for a bathroom floor. You can also organize towels in vintage containers. I use an old locker basket on top of the cabinet to stack them for display. If you have cute towels, why not let them do a little of the decorating work?

- **Monogram some totes.** I used to attach labels to the containers in my linen closet, but they always fell off because of all the humidity in the bathroom. So I decided to go the monogram tote route. I purchased super affordable monogram totes and chose a monogrammed letter for everything I wanted to organize in the space: *W* for washcloths, *A* for accessories, *S* for soap, etc. It even makes laundry day that much more fun when I fold the towels and deliver them to their charming home.

- **Create vertical organization.** I decided to make a display ladder to store items in the bathroom because when you use vertical space, it always frees up more room elsewhere. What do I store on the ladder? Extra hand soap. Tiny felted succulents. A box of extra hair ties. You know, all the usual suspects. I even stack my toilet paper vertically in a basket. Art with toilet paper. Who would have thought?

- **Pay attention to the sink area.** Remember, hooks are your friends! They help you display your towels (and use them!) and keep your sink a little cleaner. I have a hook for towels on either side of the sink.

- **Eliminate the extra.** Bathrooms tend to pick up extra stuff along the way. Count how many bottles of shampoo and conditioner are in your shower right now. I'm guessing the answer is more than two. Same with soap. And body wash. And razors. And shaving cream. And any other product you use on a regular basis. When you take out your recycling—whether it's once a week or once a month—clean out and recycle those empty containers and make your bathroom happy.

79

What Will Unite the Look of a Multipurpose Room?

I adore having a room that serves many purposes. But with those many purposes comes a lot of stuff! How do I manage the mess and chaos in a multipurpose room?

Lisa V.

Melissa says...

Ah, the blessing and curse of the multipurpose room—lots of room for various pursuits, but so much stuff that comes with those pursuits! An additional challenge is making these rooms cozy. Often you have a big empty space filled with a lot of stuff, and the room seems to lack identity and character. Because I like rooms that serve double duty, I've come up with solutions for making the space have both good form *and* function.

1   **If you have a lot of room to work with, imagine the possibilities.** See that space as an open canvas, a place where you can make your dreams happen and where people can gather, share, learn, and have fun together. Don't become overwhelmed by the possibilities.

2   **Define your space and set up activity zones and destination corners.** What will the primary functions of this room be? Will it be used for reading and study? Is it a place for aspiring musicians to practice? Do you need to devote a significant amount of space to artwork and creative pursuits? Will a Bible study or a book group be meeting regularly in this area? Will you spend time playing games and watching movies together? Choose a few functions and then set up the room around those.

3   **Create peaceful corners.** Even if one of the main purposes of the room is functioning as a gathering space for small-group meetings, movie marathons, and board game competitions, you still need a little corner for your introverts and quiet seekers to hang out. I've devoted a corner of my gathering room to be a reading corner destination. A dust-free glass cabinet for books and a comfortable settee were just right for this space. The corner offers an invitation to relax, and even if we don't have time to sit down right then, the peace of the corner invites us to eventually slow down and breathe.

4   **If any space could benefit from a cleaning frenzy, this is it!** Make it a regular thing to invite all family members into the multipurpose room, set a timer for 15 minutes, and challenge yourselves to a 15-minute transformation. Here's a fun idea: Take before and after pictures of the space. Then reward yourself with takeout, a movie, a board game, or another treat. It's a creative and effective way to make memories and keep the room tidy!

5 Organize, organize, organize! Use boxes, baskets, crates, buckets, and shelves to keep like items together. Search thrift stores, IKEA, and other discount stores for economical storage options that will work for your various needs and your style preference. Anything can be corralled in a container—colored pens, books, movies, board games, blankets, craft supplies. If you have kids, keep in mind that you can place your family focus on having less random stuff (toys and electronics) and provide more intentional opportunities to create and learn new skills through actual activities (building things, reading, drawing, painting, playing board games, cooking, caring for pets, exploring outdoors).

6 Determine a place for everything and then commit to that choice. The routine of placing used or moved items back in their assigned spots might not stick the first week or even month, but the more accustomed you and your family become to putting things back in the cupboard, on the shelf, or in the crate, the better able you are to preserve and enjoy the space. When clutter in one area gets the best of you, set a timer for 15 to 30 minutes and get all those random items back to their designated storage homes. Done!

80

My Family Uses the Family Room...So There's *That*.

There's a major mess happening in my family room. It's the go-to place for family projects, homework sessions, movie marathons, and game nights. But it's also the go-to place for all the stuff that doesn't have a home elsewhere in the house—including all the off-season holiday decorations. How can I attempt to bring order to this room?

Sarah P.

KariAnne says...

Ah, *that* room! You might call it the family room. Or the bonus room. Or the multipurpose room. Me? I call it the imagination room. It's where my family lives and hopes and dreams. The challenge? Sometimes all the chaos and clutter gets in the way of living. Keeping the room clean and organized is easy if you start with a few basic organizational principles.

The first thing to do is designate a few main purposes for your imagination room. What are the main pursuits that happen there? Maybe it's crafting sessions, game nights, and Lego-creating marathons. Or homework sessions, holiday gift making, and movie marathons. I recommend choosing three main activities and then setting up separate areas within the room for space to pursue your family's passions. The size of the room doesn't matter. (You might choose fewer areas for a smaller room, of course.) The size of the imagination does.

Next, look for a space you can reclaim that you might have otherwise overlooked. For example, when we moved into our house, we remodeled a space under the stairs just off the family room. We painted it white, and then I kind of forgot about it. One day I rediscovered it, cleaned it out, and added some fun organizing components. I cleared all the nonsense off the shelves and created a gift-wrapping station and places for my home decorating supplies. I even added an area for my laptop and transformed the space into an office.

Looking for some organizational ideas to get you started in your space? Here are some of my favorite tips:

- Baskets are my go-to organizing companion—glorious, wonderful, incredible baskets you can't see through. They simplify the look while hiding the piles and the mess. I use them for "in" and "out" boxes. Using a clothespin, I clip a marquee letter on the front of each basket (*A* for incoming and *Z* for outgoing). This looks so much neater than the pile of papers that was there before.

- For my to-do list, I used an old shutter and clipped my to-do notepad to the shutter with a clothespin. You could also add sticky notes to the shutter. Or important reminders. Cute—and very easy to clean up.

- Two filing cabinets, a tabletop, and a decorative metal basket make the ideal gift-wrapping station. Organize your rolls of wrapping paper in the basket, use the flat surface of the tabletop when you're wrapping the gifts, and store all your other supplies in the filing cabinets.

- I hung a metal scissor rack on the wall to store (and display!) all my gorgeous ribbons. I used to keep them in a bin, but now I can see everything I have. It saves me time, and it adds so much to the room.

- My reclaimed space under the stairs is small, so I just added a simple wooden chair to create a desk for my laptop. You can paint the chair to match the space, and it will look as if it always belonged there.

- My favorite way to store office supplies is in galvanized tins. They fit my home's farmhouse look while keeping everything organized and easy to find.

- One final organizing idea? A rolling basket. These can be a little pricey, but they're worth every cent. They're ideal for the extra blankets and pillows every imagination room needs.

81

Can Function and Beauty Work Together in a Home Office?

I see beautiful photos of home offices, and I have no idea how people actually work in them! My home office always has projects in process and out in the open. How can I decorate this space so it has attractive form and real function?

Amber H.

Melissa says...

I'm right there with you! So many projects, so little time—it's a challenge to keep an office clean and organized. Especially when it's a *home* office and tends to collect items that belong in other rooms of the house. (Hello, dishes and laundry!) The good news is that you don't have to have a lot of square feet to have a functional office.

I'm not a naturally organized person, so without some intentional measure of order I'm a stressed-out disaster. I've had to learn how to organize myself and my things. The key is to utilize your space to its fullest potential and give it a healthy dose of charm and personality too.

Think about the purposes you need to fulfill and make decisions from there. My work involves two seemingly opposite daily functions: creativity and business. I have the writing, photography, and design side of things, and I have the less glamorous work of managing spreadsheets or doing taxes. Whatever functions you determine as your priorities, these ideas should serve you well.

1 **Choose furniture that suits your needs and your personal style.** I didn't head to a furniture supply store when it came time to choose pieces for my home office space. It was important to me to choose pieces that fit my style, flowed well with my home, and offered order and beauty. Wherever you carve out your work space, I recommend including furniture and accessories that serve and support you and your dreams. My desk is paired with a secondhand antique secretary and a painted white hutch, where I store paint swatches, special books, computer and camera gadgets, and a variety of fun things. I use the pull-down desk part as a secondary surface for a laptop or even to serve snacks! Make sure your office chair is comfy as well as attractive. It doesn't have to match the desk. It just has to feel right to you.

2 **Give yourself motivation and tools to stay organized.** Shelving units are a must for organizing your home office. Try to go vertical as much as possible while still leaving some breathing space. I like rectangular baskets for storing items such as papers,

notebooks, file folders, and other supplies. Add cute labels to keep yourself happy and organized.

3 **Create stations that will help with work flow, productivity, and organization.** Maintain order by designating areas or certain pieces of furniture for particular tasks. I divide up my spaces into stations for paper and mail, technology, creative supplies, and even coffee for an inspiring beverage break. If you don't have a full room as an office, still apply this principle by making certain shelves and drawers into stations.

4 **Preserve some white space.** Even if you have a lot to cram into a small area, do your best to give yourself some clear space on your desk, shelving, or walls so you feel the breathing room and inspiration of white space. You'll appreciate this when you are under a deadline or overwhelmed.

5 **Put your personal stamp on the space.** Always add in objects and décor touches that represent your personality: a vase of your favorite flowers, a cute and cozy lamp, cherished family photos. Bring the spirit of home into the office. The best part of having a home office is the fact that you get to make it a reflection of who you are, how you work best, and the dreams you are working toward.

82

I Need a Post-Holiday Pep Talk (and Tips)!

I'm super on top of things during the Christmas season, but when the holidays are over and it's time to put things away, everything is just a huge mess— and I have no energy left to deal with it. Do you have any tips?

Jane C.

KariAnne says...

I so hear you! My house may look like a showroom after I'm done with my initial decorating, but come take a look after the yearly Christmas celebration is in the books. The entryway itself is a hot mess. It's auditioning for an episode of *Entryways Gone Wild*. You would find bits of paper and ribbon and tags and empty stockings and a reindeer wearing a party hat and sunglasses. Here's how I don't let all that paper and the reindeer intimidate me.

1. **Don't completely un-decorate.** Some of your décor is Christmas disguised as winter. Christmas snowflakes can become winter snowflakes. Reindeer are winter forest creatures. Tabletop trees are winter flora and fauna. Twinkle lights are just like stars in the sky. A lot of your Christmas decorations can hang around until March.

2. **Choose cute organizers.** It's a proven algebraic formula. The cuter the organizer, the greater the chance you will actually use it.

3. **Label it.** I use this tip every single day for every single season. Sometimes things are lying around the house and have no idea where to go—like a reindeer wearing a party hat and sunglasses. You have to help them out, and that's where cute tags come into play. (Well, you don't have to label the reindeer, but you get the idea.)

4. **Put away the projects.** We all have handmade projects we were eventually going to get to: the knitted items, the quilted treasures, even the store-bought Christmas cards. If you didn't get to them before Christmas, you're probably not going to get to them now. (And hey, there's always next year!)

5. **Return the books.** If you're a regular library user, chances are you checked out some favorite Christmas stories. Avoid the overdue fines and get those books back to the library.

6 **Declutter as you store away.** Make it a rule that you need to get rid of at least as many items as you add. Now is a terrific time to sort through closets and drawers. Did your family receive three new board games under the tree? Choose at least three games you've outgrown or never really got into playing and send them on their way.

7 **Pare down if you stock up.** While post-Christmas sales are a great time to stock up on next year's decorations, let some of the old ones go before you pack away the boxes in storage. If you have to keep buying new storage containers each year, that's a problem. You can stock up, but only if you also pare down.

83

How Can I Simplify Decorating All Year?

I'm trying to balance my seasonal décor so that I don't have too much going on in any one season. I'm fairly organized with my Christmas decorating, but what about the other times of the year? How can I stay on top of decorating so that it doesn't look messy and disorganized, especially during transitional times?

Brenda B.

KariAnne says...

As much as I adore seasonal decorating, I've noticed that the season tends to show up when I'm not even looking for it. Like when I was at the dollar store stocking up on dish detergent and tortillas and last-minute Fourth of July flags—and I saw an entire basket of white chocolate pumpkin candy. Pumpkins? In July? (Of course I bought a package!) I guess the moral of the story here is to always be prepared. You never know when you're going to find the right decorating item at the right price—and I can guarantee it will probably be during the wrong season. Now that we have that established, I'm going to share what's always on my radar for spring, summer, fall, and winter decorating. These are classic pieces that won't grow tired after a season or two.

SPRING

When I first moved to the country, I attended a canning class. Truly, I had no idea what I was in for. I'm not sure how much I learned, but suffice to say I left the class with

my tail between my legs and two jars of tomatoes. And now I use mason jars to decorate—especially in the spring.

- Fill the jars with limes or lemons and then add water and fresh-cut flowers from the yard.

- If one mason jar is amazing, why not seven? Stack them in a galvanized metal stand for a tiered centerpiece.

- Place mason jars inside wire baskets and group them together for a spring-y mantel display.

SUMMER

Sometimes you need to change up just one or two things to refresh a room for the new season.

- Add a few summery-patterned pillows or accessories, such as swirls and twists and flowers and leaves.

- Garden going crazy? Use it for decorating! A bowl of bright red tomatoes. Jars of crisp green cucumbers-turned-pickles.

- Refresh the bedrooms. Bring out your lightest cotton sheets and your sheer curtains. Add a vase of flowers to every bedside table.

FALL

You're going to see a theme here. (Hint: It has to do with what I found at the dollar store. And it's not chocolate.)

- A little orange is your friend. Normally orange and I don't run in the same circles, but for fall? It's perfect.

- Look for texture. Let's take pumpkins, for example (surprise, surprise!). You can find jute pumpkins and toile pumpkins and galvanized metal pumpkins and wood pumpkins. (And white chocolate pumpkins.)

- There's something about a little cotton—in a wreath or mixed in with twigs from the yard or grouped together in a vase—that makes a display a little more fall.

WINTER

When we think of winter decorating, it's easy to think Christmas. But remember Christmas décor can become winter décor. Think neutral colors and textural pieces replacing the santas, the stockings, and light up blinking Christmas sign.

- Try a simple DIY, take pinecones and glue them onto a piece of reclaimed wood in the shape of a snowflake.

- Spray paint twigs white to make a winter wreath.

- Take the ribbons or bows off your garlands and allow that greenery to shine on its own.

Now that you have the ideas and the creative suggestions for seasonal decorating, here are a few ideas to keep all those decorating elements organized.

1   Select a tub color for each season. For example, red totes might be for Christmas, white totes might be for spring, orange totes might be for fall, and so on. This makes it easy to find your décor with a glance.

2   Label the totes on the inside cover. Make a list of the contents of the tub on a piece of paper and tape it to the inside of the lid.

3   Take a photo. If you like a particular display you created, take a photo and tape it to the lid of the tub with all the coordinating accessories. That way you can easily recreate it next year.

4   Get creative by repurposing everyday items. For example, use egg crates to hold ornaments, plastic cups to hold smaller décor items, leftover cut cardboard tubes to hold wrapping paper in place, and even small shoeboxes to hold ribbons and trim.

Accessories & Styling

After you've done the big stuff—painting the walls, installing new flooring, arranging your furniture and rugs—you may still feel your home is unfinished. Nothing is more frustrating than being close to the decorating finish line and yet still feeling as if you need to run a mile. You love the shades and patterns and textures you've chosen, and everything *should* look pulled together at this point—but something seems to be missing.

That something missing is often all of the accessories and final design details. You've created a good, basic canvas. You just need to add a little more "you." Now is the time to pull out the items you love—all the items that have meaning and history and purpose to you. And then? Decorate with them to give your home that one-of-a-kind, personalized stamp. The process can be fun and frustrating all at the same time, but with a few reminders and imaginative ideas, you can eliminate the frustration and embrace the fun.

84

I'm Ready for Accessories. Now What?

I've completed the big projects, and I'm ready to focus on the actual decorating with accessories. I'm eager to get going on my rooms and even my front porch, but I get stuck knowing where to start. How do I take that first step when I'm overwhelmed just thinking about choosing a few furnishings or accessories?

Patricia P.

KariAnne says...

Congratulations! Finishing the biggest projects is the hardest part. You got the rest. Truth? The best part about decorating your home is creating your own unique style. Start slowly by layering in things you love to your spaces. A home isn't decorated in a day. Take your time to create spaces that are truly yours. Ready to get started? Here are ten easy decorating tips to help you take those first decorating steps:

1   **Remember the ottoman.** I used to have a coffee table, but everyone kept putting their stinky socks on it. Out with the coffee table, in with a tufted ottoman. To create a flat surface on the ottoman, I added a DIY wood tray as a stacking space for random books and a place to show off flowers from the yard.

2   **Built-ins are your friend.** Built-ins are an affordable option when furniture doesn't seem to fit. An inexpensive option for built-ins is to start with basic, unfinished kitchen cabinets and build around them. It's a custom look for half the price.

3   **Accept your kitchen right where it is.** It doesn't have to be high-end with all the latest appliances and time-saving gadgets. Clever storage options, faux stone laminate, updated hardware, and a kitchen island made out of a table are just a few ways to update your kitchen on a budget.

4   **Your tile doesn't have to be fancy.** I couldn't afford expensive tile, so I went with 79-cent subway tile. To give it a high-end look, I added a smaller beaded tile to update the inexpensive subway tile and create visual interest.

5   **Create a chalkboard.** True fact: There's a potential chalkboard project behind every corner at the thrift store. Paint the center of an old frame, a tray, or a crate. I've even painted the inside of an old billiard cue frame I found at a junk store. You can also paint a chalkboard surface directly onto the wall in a hallway or family gathering space.

6 Make a pillow. Pillows are a simple and easy way to update a room. Here are a couple of easy no-sew DIY ideas: Tie pompoms onto a knit pillow. Paint a quote on the front of a pillow. Cut out a silhouette of a person (or your house) and glue it on a basic pillow form.

7 Build a recipe wall. This is one of my all-time favorite projects, and you can find DIY instructions on my blog. It's so easy to make and a great conversation starter.

8 Embrace the imperfect. My tables and chairs and other furniture pieces have earned every single ding and scratch. They're a testament to the active life my family leads in our home, and I wouldn't have it any other way. I never apologize for all the imperfections. I embrace them and add a few more nicks along the way.

9 Every house needs a little blue and white. Neutrals are my favorite. They are a great foundation and go with absolutely everything. But every now and then there is such joy in embracing color.

10 Create a place to sit in the sunshine. Everyone needs a little outdoor space to call their own, whether it's a wraparound porch or a cozy little backyard deck.

How Do I Showcase the Things I Love?

I've completely tidied my home and I love it. What should I consider when surrounding myself with the things I love in regard to the composition, shape, and color story of displayed items so they shine?

Janice A.

Melissa says...

My bit of wisdom to offer is to really enjoy the clean and clear spaces. You've given yourself a great opportunity to allow your rooms to breathe and to take stock of what you really need.

Resist the urge to refill the newly emptied spaces with brand-new accessories and decorative items. Many of the items you might decide to showcase and add to your settings and surfaces can already be found in your home. Sometimes they just need to move to a new space. And maybe you don't really need to add much at all—or add items gradually, as they become meaningful to you.

When you display only the items you truly love—items that have meaning or purpose in your life—your home will be well decorated *and* tell a story at the same time. Be selective when you're shopping for new items or rediscovering them in your own home.

Use styles, colors, and patterns that inspire you. What colors feel the most peaceful to you? Limit your hues to a few shades in that color family to create a soothing palette. Keep your accessorizing simple with unfilled surfaces.

Did you know that some of the items you and your family reach for everyday can function as some of your most artful accessories? For example, you can decorate your kitchen with dishes, pitchers, mugs and teacups, kitchenware, plates, baskets, and serving trays. It might sound silly to use the term *decorate* in regard to these everyday household items, but when your practical items are in colors and patterns you love, you might find you don't have a need for as many purely decorative pieces. I'd rather splurge on a few gorgeous mugs than find room for a dozen ho-hum mugs that I don't love and then attempt to add accessories that aren't useful to jazz things up.

Keep your decorative elements simple, focus on making your everyday accessories beautiful, and you'll find peace and joy in a home you love.

I Want Pretty Things Now (and Cheap)…Is That a Problem?

I'm the ultimate impatient decorator. I want to achieve a styled-over-time look, but I want the look I want NOW! Because I don't have a large budget for decorating, I've been working to become an avid garage saler and thrift shopper. How can I find attractive but inexpensive items that still make my entire home look classy and put together?

Melissa S.

KariAnne says...

Most of us don't have the means to select our favorite items from an upscale home decorating retailer, put them all in our shopping cart (virtual or otherwise), and call it a decorating day. And when you think about it, what would be the fun in that? Sure, everything might match and coordinate and look absolutely fabulous together, but where is the *you* in that style of decorating? And where is the fun—the joy of happening upon the perfect piece, the amazement at that incredible find, the boost of confidence when you combine the most unlikely items into an artful display?

We were all created by God to be unique, and we need to let our homes reflect that. Every one of us was designed by an amazing, incredible, awe-inspiring Creator. In this entire world, there's no one else quite like us. We each have our own style. Our own likes and dislikes. Our own individual perspective. And we can confidently and joyfully reflect those truths in our homes.

Now that I've given you the be-an-original pep talk, here are my favorite find-an-original tips for discovering treasures on the cheap:

1 **Make a list of three things you always want to watch for at yard sales and thrift shops.** This will help give you focus in an overwhelming environment. You might choose books, milk glass, and white dishes. (I know I would.)

2 **Keep an eye out for containers.** Bowls, baskets, vases, buckets, crates, trays, goblets, pitchers—all of these are fair game. Many can be easily upgraded with a coat of paint. Or you can turn a chipped or stained side to the wall. (On the other hand, chips and other imperfections add character to an item.) Something that holds something else always serves a purpose, and these items are so versatile as you move them from room to room. You also can't go wrong with classic pieces in classic shapes.

3 **Picture frames are super easy to alter.** Spray paint comes in so many shades and finishes. Really, you can achieve practically any look with spray paint. Also look beyond the photo currently taking up

residence in the thrift shop frame. All you need to do is remove it and replace it with your own photo, a piece of artwork, or even a free design found online and printed from your computer.

4   Don't pass up fun little knickknacks. While you want to avoid clutter, you can also show your sense of humor and put your personality on display. Just select what appeals to you personally and try out what makes you smile. Don't overthink it.

5   Always, always look for mirrors. You can add them to any room. They'll reflect light and make any space brighter and more welcoming. Display them on the walls, lean them on the mantel, or add them to your flat surfaces. Mirrors make anything look better.

87

How Do I Own My Style While Renting?

How can I best decorate an apartment where I'm not allowed to paint the walls or make any nail holes? I am young, recently married, and trying to save money for our dream home. I want to make our apartment a beautiful space, but I'm a little stunted by the rules.

Bernice T.

Melissa says...

While apartment rules can seem like limitations, they are actually blessings in disguise. When every penny counts, you'll be happy you're not tempted to spend money on costly changes like new flooring or cabinetry. You have the freedom to focus on what you *can* do—which is quite a lot!

- **Decorate your bathroom first.** It's a small, manageable space, and it's amazing what a few changes can do. A colorful new shower curtain, some fluffy towels in coordinating colors, a mirrored tray displaying your favorite beauty products, and you're good to go.

- **Bring in the outdoors with potted plants.** From large plants that sit on the floor to tiny succulents that adorn a windowsill, greenery in colorful planters brings a pop of color and style to any space.

- **Refresh your bedding.** It's easy to find sheets, pillows, blankets, and comforters on sale at discount home goods stores. Bedding in your favorite color or pattern will make your bedroom feel comfortable at night and pulled together during the day, even when you forget to make the bed. (Have you noticed how many beds are unmade in home decorating catalogs and on store websites? Really, it's a thing!)

- **Put pillows everywhere!** They aren't just for the bed. Toss them on chairs and sofas—and you can even store extra pillows in a big basket. To save space, buy or make pillow covers to switch out seasonally.

- **Call in a rug to the rescue.** If your existing carpet or flooring makes you cringe, this is a simple fix. Rugs give any room an entirely different look and feel while softening the space and providing a cozier vibe. Put a small rug by your bed, in a bathroom, or in front of the sink, or use it to create style in a living room or dining room when layered with a larger rug.

- **Invest in tools for organization.** Purchase a new set of clothes hangers (like the thin, velvety variety—it's amazing how much more closet space those free up!). Wire or cloth baskets help you keep track of just about anything—socks, cosmetics, kitchen items. Use

what you can to keep a small space streamlined and clutter-free.

- **Frame encouraging words.** Nothing can make an apartment feel more like home than frames with inspirational messages displayed inside. Your favorite quotes from books or scriptures are available at craft stores or can even be printed for free from the internet. Frames are inexpensive, versatile, and can be easily updated as your style grows and changes.

- **Display art creatively.** Set art on a mantel, a shelf, a desk, or a table and lean it against the wall to display it without creating nail holes. Look into alternative picture holders that will avoid wall damage.

- **Focus on your dreams.** Put up an inspiration board with pictures of your dream home to keep you motivated to save money and to keep discovering the style you love.

- **Stay thankful.** Notice the gifts of the place you live in right now. Even when you can't spend much money or make dramatic changes to your rooms, your efforts to express your personal style and appreciating what you have will result in a home you love.

- **Invest in your future.** Your choices now will impact your options tomorrow. So use what you have, shop for sales, and avoid spending money on accessories or furniture you don't think you'll want or like later.

88

How Do I Balance Sentiment and Style?

I feel most comfortable in a home decorated with family pictures and other personal objects. Anything that reminds me of times with family gives meaning to an object and to my home. How can I do this and still make my house and style look nice?

Mayola G.

Melissa says...

Photos and art pieces give your home heart and soul and spark conversation as they tell chapters of your story. And what better story to tell than the story of family? Nothing personalizes a room better than one-of-a-kind photos and family treasures. You can definitely strike the balance between preserving family memories and achieving a gorgeous decorating style. Here are a few tips to help you do that:

1   Bring the world into your home. Choose your favorite photos, sketches, drawings, paintings, and even mementos (like tickets or programs) from your travels to decorate your home and bring back memories of time spent together in beautiful places.

2   Create space for special photos. If you have a table or desk with a protective layer of glass, consider slipping some select photos under the glass. This can be a wonderful visual display. The images are protected and are not taking up surface area.

3   **Display your favorites.** All of us have little treasures that spark special memories, but those items are often stuffed in boxes, out of sight. Use frames and shadowboxes or other display techniques to showcase items of value: your daughter's newborn hat, a meaningful piece of jewelry, your grandmother's favorite linens. You could even create a gallery wall of special pieces.

4   **Let your memories shine.** Do you have a million photos on your phone or computer but none on your walls? Make a commitment to print out favorite photos, and then frame and display them. You can purchase inexpensive frames at IKEA or thrift shops. (Spray-paint them to match your room décor if you don't care for the original frame color.) You can also add scrapbooking or art paper to create a fun and easy border. Display both color and black-and-white photos for variety. Black-and-white tend to be easier to match and put the emphasis on the photo instead of the color. In a room that has a lot of glare, consider removing the glass from the frame.

5   **Celebrate the journey.** Consider a chronological presentation of your family's journey. This is especially powerful if you have images of grandparents and great-grandparents. If you have a hallway that is wide enough so that frames can be on the walls without getting bumped, this might be the perfect place.

The heart of the home is the people who live in it, so preserving memories and telling stories matter more than any design trend. I have very little art or décor in my home that isn't directly related to a personal memory. Personal art and photos will always be right at home, whatever style of home you have.

89

What Are the Tricks to Displaying Art?

I love artwork, but I struggle figuring out how to display it.
How do I decide where to hang my art and how much art suits a room?

Melinda Y.

Melissa says...

As much as I like to dole out the do-what-you-love advice, there is an *art* to discovering your artwork display style! Remember, I'm a decorating rule breaker, and I've broken many of the rules in this area. I do, though, tend to follow a few tips when deciding how much art to bring into a room and where to place it.

- Make sure your walls have enough blank space so your eyes can rest between displays. What's right for one room or wall might be too much or too little for another.

- Decide which walls would be best blank. If you have a grand set of French doors that reveal a view you love, the wall space to the side of the door frame could easily be left alone so you don't distract from your focal point.

- Vary the number of items on each wall of a room. You don't want exactly four art pieces on all four walls. It would look better to have one gallery wall of a grid of six medium-sized frames or a gallery wall with many pieces of art next to a wall that is blank or with only one or two pieces.

- Ideally, you want to hang your artwork so it is pleasing to the eye from every angle. But don't overanalyze this.

Sometimes a piece will look fabulous from a certain angle and not as good from another. A little imperfection can make the room feel more welcoming.

- Hang everything so the midpoint of each wall vignette is within view at a similar height (usually for me that midpoint is a bit lower than my own eye level, and I'm five two). Keeping the midpoints consistent helps the art feel balanced around the room. I use a little poster putty to help keep the frames straight.

- Look beyond the walls. It's easy to change a display of artwork when it's featured on a designated art ledge. Display paintings on stands and showcase smaller pieces of art on a wire with clips (great for family creations!) or on a small table or bench.

- If in doubt, lean it! I started leaning artwork to avoid putting holes in the walls. Then I discovered I actually liked how leaning objects look. You can lean artwork on the back of bookshelves, tabletops, mantels, windowsills, floors, and stair landings. When leaning more than one item, slightly overlap each additional item in front of the piece behind it.

● After art and decorative items have been hung, leave and reenter the room to scan the space. Are the elements achieving what you want? If it feels chaotic, edit down the display. If it seems empty, add a little more. You can also modify and update as the seasons change. You might like a busy look in the winter and a barer display come summertime.

To give you courage, I'll confess to some of the rules I have happily broken! They say you can't hang art on any wall smaller than three feet wide (yes, I've broken this one). Some say you must hang art at eye level (which I generally do, except in the case of a gallery wall or over a doorway). And some say you must hang smaller frames on top of bigger frames and line everything up perfectly (broken this one too!).

What feels right and looks right for *your* space? Go with that. And trust that if you love it, it is working.

90

Can I Really Take Photos Worth Displaying?

I love homes that are filled with gorgeous, professional-looking family and vacation and nature photos. I'd like to display favorite pictures on my own walls, but I'm not a professional and I can't afford to hire a professional photographer. Can you give me some tips for taking better photos?

Kimberley O.

KariAnne says...

You can take classes and read books and articles, but really, the best way to become a good photographer is through trial and error. Yes, the quality of your camera and lens counts, and yes, some people have a natural eye for composition, but with a few pointers and some practice, you can take gorgeous pictures that are gallery wall worthy.

1 **Manually focus.** I know it's scary. I get it. But it's kind of like learning to like broccoli. At first it looks all green and vegetable-y, but after a while you're adding it by the handful to your stir-fry pasta. And liking it. Mastering the manual focus gives you control. You're the boss who tells the camera what to focus on, instead of the other way around. And it's actually pretty easy. Simply flip the switch on the side of the lens to manual. Then move the focus box around until you've established the area of your photo you want to bring into focus. Then move the focus dial until the picture is in perfect focus. There, that wasn't so bad, was it?

2 **Use a tripod.** No brainer, right? But...not all tripods are created equal. My $200 photography store tripod yields significantly better results than my discount store tripod. It's an investment, but the sharper pictures make it worthwhile. A tripod, of course, holds your camera steady, which prevents movement when you take a picture. The result? Sharp, in-focus photos.

3 **Try PicMonkey or any other editing tool.** I like PicMonkey because it's not fancy, plus it's almost free. It comes with tons of free features for me to use, like the sharpening tool. I just upload a picture, edit away, and reduce or enlarge it to the desired size. Just before I save it, I sharpen it. (I always make sure that sharpening is the very last thing I do.) The editing process sometimes takes something away from the picture and can change the sharpness of the photo. By sharpening at the end, my pictures always look crisper and cleaner.

4 Get the proper lighting. Photos taken in low light or with a higher ISO tend to look grainy. And grainy pictures will never look sharp, no matter how much you click the sharpen button on your editing tool. Yes, I learned this the hard way. I took all these pictures for a magazine once with my ISO set to 3200 by accident. When I went to edit the photos, I could not sharpen them no matter what trick I tried. Lesson learned. Always get the proper lighting.

5 Set the timer. Cameras come equipped with a built-in timer that allows you to delay taking the picture by seconds. (You can also purchase an external remote attachment that plugs into your camera.) A timer prevents the camera from moving even the slightest bit. Sometimes when you click the button, you accidentally move the camera just a little. The remote or the camera timer ensures your camera will stay still.

91

What Are Design Basics for a Gallery Wall?

I'm excited to get going creating gallery walls for my home. I'd like to display favorite photos along with other artwork and collected finds. How can I create displays that draw attention yet are artfully arranged without looking too cluttered?

Nancy M.

KariAnne says...

If you have a blank wall—or multiple blank walls—in your home, please come sit by me. I have a few blank walls of my own I'd like you to meet.

Gallery walls are a great choice to fill up a wall like this—but where do you start? Do you have the right mix of photos and frames? Are you arranging them the right way? Do you need to add more than photos to your display? What about architectural pieces or wall quotes or monograms or a wreath? Should you add those too? Will those items coordinate as well?

I'm always decorating my walls, and in the process I've learned a thing or two about gallery walls and what makes them tick besides clocks. Looking to transform your blank wall? Why not create a gallery wall with some of these personalized art ideas?

1 **Add a creative touch.** Have a mathematician in the family? Create a reclaimed wood sign that consists of the first 100 digits of pi.

2 **Go crafty.** Looking for a creative DIY plate display? Start with a vinyl design found at a craft store.

Lay the design over a collection of white plates. Next, cut out pieces of the design for each plate. Then hang the plates on the wall to recreate the original design.

3 **Budget for beauty.** Create a one-of-a-kind mirror from dollar store compacts. Divide each compact in half. Next, place the compacts onto a wood circle to form a mirror. Glue each compact in place.

4 **Add fun and function.** Paint an extra wall in your space with chalkboard paint. This is a great way to turn an empty wall into a conversation starter. Especially if someone starts the conversation with chalk.

5 **Let words inspire.** Reclaim some old boards and stencil your favorite sayings on them. You can display a word, a favorite verse, or even a fun life lesson.

6 **Put a pin in it.** If you're worried about damaging your walls—or you rent a home where you're not allowed to nail anything to the walls—create a gallery wall on a floating pegboard instead.

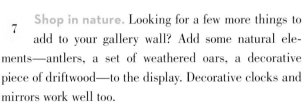

7 **Shop in nature.** Looking for a few more things to add to your gallery wall? Add some natural elements—antlers, a set of weathered oars, a decorative piece of driftwood—to the display. Decorative clocks and mirrors work well too.

8 **Maximize spaces.** Instead of a gallery wall, what about a gallery corner? Wrap the photos, artwork, and monograms around the corner of your room. This is an ideal solution if you're lacking wall space.

9 **Start with a statement.** A good rule of thumb for designing your gallery wall: Begin with a statement piece or pieces and design the rest of the wall from there. Lay your items on the ground and see what stands out. Then center everything else around that.

10 **Switch it up a bit.** Paint the wall behind your gallery display a brilliant color. Black-and-white photos contrast well with jewel tones and darker shades of color. To make the display pop, keep your frame choices sleek and simple.

11 **Keep it cozy.** When displaying artwork and photos, avoid too much space between each frame. Frames hung closer together look more curated.

92

Mirror, Mirror on My Wall… And Where Else?

I love the look of mirrors in my home. How can I incorporate them into the various rooms in my house?

Luby B.

Melissa says...

I'm with you. I love decorating with mirrors! At one point I probably had a dozen mirrors sitting on the floor of my house, leaning against the walls, and just waiting for all the remodeling to be done so I could finally hang them up. (Yes, I have a problem with mirrors—and I especially adore round mirrors.) I love using them to make sure I look cute before I head out the door, but I mostly love them for how they reflect light and add to the mood of our home. Mirrors can make a statement and set the style in any room in your house.

1   **When using more than one mirror in a room, vary the sizes.** One large mirror in a room is enough to be a statement piece (unless you are intentionally using a pair of matching mirrors over twin beds or a sofa). Additional mirrors on other walls should be smaller in size, grouped together as a collection or gallery wall, or different shapes.

2   **Remember the design rule of three.** (While I'm not big on rules, this one helps you know where to place a decorative item like a mirror.) Mirrors hung above a sofa or a bed should be about two-thirds the width of what is below. (This is a good tip to follow when hanging artwork as well.)

3 **Don't rule out vintage mirrors!** Often it just takes a good cleaning to make a secondhand shop find the perfect fit for your home.

4 **Every small space can benefit from the addition of a mirror.** Any light that streams into the space will be reflected by the mirror, and the depth of the image from the reflection will make your space look bigger.

5 **Use mirrored trays to hold items.** These look gorgeous in the bathroom holding favorite lotions and perfumes and create a spa-like ambience. You can also add a mirrored tray to the coffee table or the dining room table.

6 **If you can't install a window in a room, try hanging a mirror instead.** I love round mirrors for accomplishing a similar look. Round mirrors are one of my favorite accessories to add a circular shape, reflect light, and add interest to a room.

7 **A mirror hung above the bed makes a classic statement.** Look for creative shapes and frames that add a unique touch.

8 **Hang a mirror above an entryway table to open up the room** and provide a window-like look to ease the transition from indoors to outdoors (and vice versa!). I love the look of plants and flowers reflected in an entryway mirror.

9 **Hang bathroom mirrors at the correct level for people using the space.** If those using the bathroom are of varying heights, get a large enough mirror for everyone to see their reflection.

10 **A mirror hung above the fireplace is a traditional look,** but also consider adding a mirror to the dining room wall or in the kitchen for an unexpected but space-expanding touch.

93

Can My Décor Secret Be an Open Book?

Books are such an important part of my life.
How can I incorporate my book collection into my decorating scheme?

Kim G.

Melissa says...

We are kindred spirits. And we're so lucky that our favorite treasures can be enjoyed as a decorating accessory. It makes me happy to glance around the house and see the varied tones and textures of the book spines and covers. Inspiration and practicality bound in attractive colors—what more could we ask for?

Our printed prizes can be shown in any room in a variety of ways. Here is my favorite advice based on years of moving my treasured books from place to place.

- **Get display ideas from bookstores.** Who doesn't want a research field trip to a bookstore? Notice how the retailer combines and lines up books on shelves, especially in the areas where they showcase their first editions or featured specials.

- **Use books to add warmth to other accessories.** Mix several of your favorite things together. Tuck a vintage book in with your displayed collection of calligraphy pens or paperweights. Add a stack or two in a glass cabinet that holds mugs, plates, and pitchers for an unexpected yet perfect effect. Place a globe next to a grouping of books for a cozy and collegiate look. Other

display options: gather books in a basket, use a stack as a foundation for an accessory, place a special volume on a wicker tray near the couch, or present an entire series between bookends of stone, bronze, or wood for an extra touch of texture in any room.

- **Bring books into your seasonal decorating.** A gardening guide next to a potted daffodil in the spring, a vintage book of hymns or Christmas carols beside a silver bell in December...the ideas are endless.

- **Don't let anyone tell you that books are clutter.** If you want to organize all your books by color or subject, go for it. But if that's too much effort, not to worry. Enjoy rearranging them for an impact of color or to bring a theme to light. No matter how they are displayed, they really are works of art—the typography, the artwork, the colors, and the covers as well. You can easily have books as part of the décor in any room—even the kitchen. On my shelves, among my kitchen accessories and essentials, are various cookbooks, gardening books, and entertaining books. In my opinion, where there is a room, there is room for books! And no bedroom is complete without a "to-read" cache on the nightstand placed beside a pretty lamp and a cup of tea. It really doesn't get any cozier than that!

- **Use interior pages for interior design.** The next time you are at an antique store, ask if they have loose pages from vintage books. Sometimes you will come across a page or cover from a picture book you loved as a child or a classic adventure tale your family has read for generations. Frame a few pages individually or as a

larger collage for a striking signature piece. Use pages to line a book shelf or a small display cupboard. You see? Books keep on giving to your home's style, ambience, and character.

Versatile and meaningful, books tell a story in their pages, and they tell a story about you and your family. They make a space personal. Their very presence weaves the tale of what you find beautiful and what you love to read, learn about, and share with people you care about.

94

When Is an Arrangement Just Right?

How do you know when a space (a bookshelf, a coffee table, a centerpiece) is finished being styled? I always feel I need to keep adding more, but then my display ends up being way too cluttered. Help!

Heather S.

KariAnne says...

In your quest for a put-together, happily-ever-after ending, don't rule out one of the joys of decorating: the freedom to be forever puttering, changing, and transitioning. While it can give you a satisfying sense of accomplishment to see that forever-in-process room finally come together, allow yourself to see your home as a work in progress. Now, I don't mean you have to have paint-splattered drop cloths on the floor for years or empty picture frames forever filling the countertops. Definitely work toward completion. But in the decorating and the accessorizing, continue to mix things up to keep your design fresh and fun. Because I love yard sales and thrift shops so much, I like to keep myself open to new possibilities. Two of my favorite recent design projects include a stylish coffee table redo and a novel bookcase redesign.

COFFEE TABLE

To style a coffee table, I always start with something low, such as a basket, tray, or platter. Then I stack books or group objects that are different heights. You want to make sure to vary the silhouette of your display. As a final touch, add some texture—greenery or branches or wood beads all work well.

When I'm out scouring the thrift shops for new décor, I always keep an eye out for these items:

- **Old books.** It doesn't really matter what the covers look like because I cover them with scrapbook paper that matches my décor. I like to stack the covered books in groups of three and add a mason jar filled with seasonal blooms to the top of the display.

- **Low, flat baskets.** Using basic alphabet stencils and craft paint, I stencil something fun, like our family name and the year our house was built. You could also add an inspirational word, a Bible verse, or a favorite saying. I place the basket in the center of the coffee table and fill it with books and magazines.

- **Wooden trays.** I paint these or decorate them to match the season and then fill them with different sizes of grapevine spheres or other decorations. A small string of battery-powered fairy lights looks pretty here too.

BOOKCASE

A bookcase also makes an ideal backdrop for decorating inspiration. Whenever I style a bookcase, I start from scratch and remove everything from the shelves. Then I stack books in the bookcase. (Novel concept, right? Pun totally intended.) I recommend placing five to seven books on one side of the shelf and then five to seven books on the other side, leaving a little breathing space. Occasionally I turn two books on their sides at the end of each row of books and add decorative accessories to the empty spots. Sometimes I also place trays or baskets behind the books to achieve additional height.

As I said, I'm always collecting and consequently never quite finished with my decorating. And that's okay! It brings me such joy to design and create, and I can't imagine being finished and done. Besides, I wouldn't have an excuse to keep visiting yard sales and thrift shops!

95

Which Natural Elements Are Ideal Accessories?

I would love to bring the outdoors into my home. What are your tips for using and enjoying items from nature as part of my décor?

Daisy R.

Melissa says...

Sometimes you literally stumble upon the perfect décor in the most unexpected places. My husband and I were out walking one rainy day in a small forested area near our home. In a less than graceful move, I attempted to leap over a stump in a big puddle to avoid slipping in the mud. As I made the long descent to the ground anyway, I happened to also stumble upon a pleasant discovery. In the clearing by the parking lot were hundreds of white birch branches scattered on the ground.

All the way home I couldn't stop talking about those branches and their decorative potential. So in the darkness of night, my husband drove back to the clearing and brought a few back for me. He's a keeper. Some branches became curtain rods, others were turned into decorative trees, and a smaller branch became a kitchen towel rod.

Adding natural elements to your home is one of the easiest and most attractive ways to decorate. And it's inexpensive and environmentally friendly too! Decorating touches brought from and inspired by the outdoors tend to be subtle and full of interesting character and texture. It doesn't get better than that. Here are some simple tips for introducing these elements into your favorite spaces:

- Most kitchens are full of cold and hard surfaces, but when you bring the outdoors in, you can warm things up. A display of beautiful flowers in a decorative pitcher adds instant charm and warmth. A bowl of oranges and lemons on the dining room table declares the bounty of the season.

- To expand on your seasonal décor, fill glass lamps or vases with pinecones, cinnamon sticks, shells, sand, moss, and some of your favorite ornaments.

- Place your garden blooms in unique containers, such as a coffee tin, a galvanized bucket, a soup tureen, an antique toolbox, or a decorative bowl.

- Take your inspiration from the sea with driftwood, shells, starfish, and even jars of sand or rocks from memorable travels.

- You can also trek to the woods to gain inspiration. Lean a tall branch in the corner of a room. Bring in branches, pinecones, moss, and other elements from the forest.

- Use simple greenery or fragrant herbs from the garden. Place a plant clipping from your yard—such as a blooming rhododendron branch—in a glass jug or jar. Air plants are an easy option and virtually impossible to kill (yay!). Plant succulents in teacups or other household containers for a pretty touch.

- It's fun to create nature-based centerpieces. Begin by choosing your container. Think creatively: pitchers, lanterns, terrariums, wood cutting boards, books, cake plates, crates, candleholders. Almost anything will do! Then select your favorite natural elements: pinecones, small plants, succulents, lemons and limes, pomegranates, acorns, pumpkins, and evergreen branches. Then, if you desire, add some fillers—moss, sprigs of greenery, small rocks, sticks, branches, flowers, sand, tiny pebbles—to finish off the look. You can even add a warm glow with a candle or some small battery-powered twinkle lights.

There are so many benefits to drawing inspiration from nature as well as shopping from nature to give your home ambience and beauty. Just think. A bouquet of flowers that was grown in your garden doesn't require any storage space when the season is over, and you can easily refresh a display that has grown tired with freshly picked blossoms. Beauty *and* function...I'm sold.

96

Are There DIYs to Design with Signs?

I love signs with sayings painted on them, but they can be quite expensive to purchase. Can you share some methods for creating these signs myself? And one more question— what do you consider to be enough when it comes to decorating with these signs?

Judy C.

KariAnne says...

I'm not sure how the signs-with-sayings trend started, but let's just say it's been a success. And I don't see it going away anytime soon. It's kind of surprising that it took this long to get going. Such a simple idea—a word painted on a sign. And then displayed. Who would have thought?

I've painted dozens of wood signs in my life. Signs and friends of signs and entire sign families. Small signs and big signs and grocery signs and signs that have only one powerful, amazing word and signs that say, "I love you." And in all my sign painting, I've learned a few things. Things that make sign painting a breeze. But there's no tip more important than this one: Start in the middle.

When I finished a master bath remodel, something was missing. Something big. So I decided to paint a giant sign for the wall. I took an existing sign that previously had said BEACH and painted a white coat over the letters. I wanted something clean and crisp, so I purchased some stencil letters, traced the letters onto the sign (which now said THISTLEWOOD FARMS EST. 1918), filled in the letters with a marker, and distressed them. It took me literally 36 minutes to finish the project. But...

One of my twins was telling me a story when I was painting the sign, and because the story was so fascinating, I stopped paying attention to my project and got off-kilter. THISTLEWOOD looked great. But FARMS? Sigh...totally messed up. All because I forgot the number one tip. Count your letters. Then start in the middle. For example, THISTLEWOOD has 11 letters, with L being the middle letter. I measured to the center of the board and placed the L there, then I went to the next two middle letters (T and E), and the letters after that S and W), and on and on until the word was perfectly centered.

My next tip? If you have the sign of your dreams in your imagination, have the confidence to create it yourself! It doesn't take much at all. You have the perfect sign in your mind, you know what colors you want it to be, and you know the exact size of the sign you need. The problem? When you go to the stores to search for the sign, you can't find it. That's because the best sign of all exists in your imagination, so you may as well paint it yourself and bring your vision to life. All it takes is some wood, paint, and your creativity. And the ability to follow the number one tip and start in the middle.

Now, about the how-many-signs-is-too-many question. That's really up to you, but realize that the fewer words you display in a room, the greater the impact of those words (or even that single word). So exercise some restraint, even if you want to go all-out in your sign painting. You can always repaint another sign when another word or thought comes to mind.

97

What Turns a Mantelpiece into a Masterpiece?

I'm stumped when it comes to decorating my mantel.
I'm not sure how many items to display—or even what kind of items to display—
and how to arrange them. I'd love any guidance you could give!

Pamela S.

KariAnne says...

While decorating your mantel can be fun, it can also be a lot of pressure. If you have a fireplace, often it's the focal point of the room. And focal points get a significant amount of attention. The good news? It's easy to change up your design. Look around the rest of the room for inspiration, take the current season of the year into consideration, and you can confidently make your mantel a work of art.

- **Mantels are a go-to choice for seasonal décor.** Christmas and Easter and spring and fall never met a mantel they didn't like. No matter the season, pay attention to three key steps to decorating your mantel: height, texture, and the rule of thirds (or fifths...or even sevenths). Start with height by displaying an oversized platter or basket. Then layer in pieces of different heights to break up the silhouette. Next, add texture to your display. Interesting choices include shiny metallic accents, woven urns, or distressed wooden planters. Finally, remember to stick with an odd number of items when arranging the display. And make sure you leave some open space for the eye to rest. Otherwise, the whole display looks too busy and cluttered.

- **It's fun to create your own garlands.** You can make a snowflake garland in the winter, flowers in the spring, starfish in the summer, or leaves in the fall. Use felt, cardstock, or whatever material catches your fancy. It's also more than okay to purchase premade garlands. Another imaginative project? Make an adorable, super simple pennant banner using triangles of seasonally appropriate fabric.

- **Plants are a popular choice and for good reason.** They balance out the brick of a fireplace nicely, and they have the added bonus of freshening the air in a room. You can also move them to a different space in your home if the mantel is temporarily taken up by an elaborate Christmas village or a display of sunflowers in late summer. A collection of three or five succulents also looks fabulous clustered on a mantel.

- **It's easy to get artsy with your mantel.** Just leaning a trio of black-and-white photos mounted in decorative frames makes a personal statement. You can also add a unique mirror (or mirrors) to brighten the space.

- **Don't be afraid to copy creative ideas.** If you see an interesting new way to display all of your candles or the perfect decorating scheme for your shell collection, copy away! If you see a picture of a vase just like the one you've been wondering how to style, go ahead and imitate that styling technique. Chances are, you don't have the exact same items, so your creation will have its own unique spin. This is actually a solid piece of advice for any decorating dilemma. Not starting from scratch can actually free you up to let your own creativity flow.

98

What Makes a Guest Suite Special?

I have a guest room I'm excited to decorate, but I'm not sure how to make it functional while letting it have personality as well. How can I accomplish both of these things?

Renee A.

Melissa says...

I love hosting guests, *and* I love being a guest. When you see things from the other side, it helps you create an environment that makes your own guests feel welcome and comfortable. Also, the experience of preparing your home for guests means your home is better prepared for you and your family's everyday life. That's a win-win all around! Don't stress about making your home perfect. It just needs to be fairly clean and comfy. Sometimes a *too-perfect* environment can actually seem cold and unwelcoming. Strive for a neutral feel to your guest room. You can include some fun pieces and adorable accessories, but guests arrive with their own belongings, and they need to feel they can fit into the room (both in terms of the physical space and in the style of decorating).

When guests are spending the night at my home, I want them to feel as if they're spending time at a cozy bed-and-breakfast. Even though my house isn't big or luxurious and I don't have a private guest wing, I can do quite a bit to make their stay memorable.

- Invest in a set of pretty sheets, and add a few extra pillows and blankets.

- Place an attractive fan in the room. Different people have different temperature needs, and it's nice to give your guests options. (Likewise, make sure they have enough heat when it's cold. Extra blankets often do the trick in this department.)

- To be sensitive to allergies and personal preferences of guests, avoid artificially perfumed and scented detergents for sheets, candles, and room sprays. It's best to strive for fresh, subtle, and natural (you can set out a pretty essential oil diffuser as an option for guests).

- Add a few current magazines or favorite books and inspirational devotionals to the bedside table for the option of nighttime reading. A coloring book and a set of colored pencils add a super cute touch. Make sure you have a good lighting source for reading (or coloring!) in bed. If you don't have room for a lamp, add a clip-on style to the side of the bed.

- A glass bottle of water on the nightstand, along with a drinking glass, is a thoughtful touch. Refill and replace as necessary.

- Put out a set of clean, fluffy towels (include wash cloths, bath towels, and hand towels) and an assortment of toiletries: shampoo, conditioner, lotion, toothpaste, new toothbrushes, disposable razors, soap, body wash, extra toilet paper, and tissues. We've all forgotten items when packing, and it's nice to have extra items at your disposal.

- My favorite accessory is always fresh flowers or a pretty plant. It's amazing how just a touch of green can make a room feel more like home.

- Clean out the dresser drawers and closet so your guests have room to hang clothes and unpack personal belongings. Guests who feel right at home tend to be easy to host.

- Frame the Wi-Fi password on the nightstand.

- Set out a pretty notebook for your guests' stay. You can include some helpful information and recommendations on local attractions and restaurants if they will be adventuring on their own. You can also use a page to let guests know about potential activities you have planned, or your daily schedule and/or menu plan so they know what to expect. Good communication always makes things go more smoothly.

99

How Can I Create an Oasis for Outdoor Entertaining?

I live in a temperate climate and adore entertaining outdoors, but I don't know the first thing to do in setting up an attractive outdoor entertaining space. Any ideas?

Tracy R.

KariAnne says...

It's easy to become so caught up in fixing up the various rooms in our homes that we completely overlook another fabulous entertaining option: our outdoor space. Sometimes this is the best entertaining alternative of all. Nature has already done most of the decorating for you, and you just need to provide the finishing touches. I live in the country, and while that has its own set of challenges (the closest Target is an hour away and the cows moo when you're trying to film a live video outside), it's a setting like no other. I like to follow these ten simple tips to ensure my outdoor entertaining is a success (with minimal stress).

1 **Feature flowers.** I always cut flowers from my yard to decorate the outdoor table. It just makes sense. I'm already outside. The flowers are right around the corner. I just wander around the yard, snipping off a few blooms or greenery or leaves or branches or whatever's currently at its peak to create the perfect centerpiece.

2 **Mismatched fits right in.** In an outdoor setting, the grass and trees don't care if your chairs match. In fact, it looks more charming if they don't. When my family eats in the backyard, we just grab any old chair and head outside.

3 **Turn up the sound track.** Music is always welcome, especially at an outdoor gathering. Nothing fancy—just a cell phone and a portable speaker. You can even create a special playlist if that's your thing (or have one of your kids create it for you). It's amazing how a little music always makes the corn taste better.

4 **Dish towels double as linens.** Paper towels at an outdoor party? Not a good idea—they blow away in the breeze. Try dish towels. They look prettier, plus you can use them to clean up the table after the party.

5 **Get imaginative with your displays.** You don't have a floor or walls or ceilings, so it's time to get creative. Hang things from the trees. I once took an old tray that had holes on the sides, hung it from jute twine, and then filled it with greenery from the yard. Fancy!

6 **Don't forget playtime.** I always want to talk to my guests after dinner, but the kids would rather be doing something else. With a little planning, I have outdoor

games ready for them, such as horseshoes or croquet or whiffle ball. That means more talking time for me!

7 **Stick with simple dishes.** I love my all-white dishes. So clean, so simple. They go with absolutely everything. Especially the outdoors.

8 **Eat beautiful.** Is there anything more gorgeous than farm-fresh fruits and vegetables? I think not. Shop farmer's markets, roadside stands, or even the organic section of the grocery store for the freshest options around.

Bonus: Grow your own garden. You can't get any fresher— or any more inexpensive—than that.

9 **Toss in some throws and pillows.** I always bring out a basket with these items. Everyone wants to stay outside longer when they can get warm and cozy. It's a terrific way to encourage more talking.

10 **Enjoy!** Don't stress. Don't worry. That's the joy of entertaining outside. If something spills, there's no need to clean it up. Just sit back, relax, and enjoy the entertaining that practically takes care of itself.

Which Seasonal Touches Are Easiest to Add In?

What are your favorite ways to update your rooms as the seasons change while still keeping your basic decorations in place? I don't want to spend too much time or money, but I like celebrating the seasons.

Bobbye J.

Melissa says...

Decorating for the seasons brings a lot of joy, and it doesn't have to be expensive or complicated. An easy way to ensure flexibility is to consider stepping away from overtly themed décor. This way you are not boxed into a look but can strike the balance between keeping things simple and mixing things up a bit each season. Use what you have, give preference to natural elements, and modify or arrange your decorations until they feel seasonally appropriate and inspiring. A glass lamp base that can be filled with pine cones one season and seashells the next is far more versatile than a ceramic one with a large image of a snowman on it.

If you go the way of simplicity, you can work with warm and cozy in the fall and winter and then lighten things up for the spring and summer months. Your basic goal really can be that simple.

One thing to consider is the seasonal style your house reflects during most of the year. I wouldn't expect you to be displaying a Christmas tree in August, but sometimes there's an obvious base seasonal style going on in your home. Fall and winter tones can be oh-so-comforting and just right for a natural or modern style. Spring and summer colors might lift your mood because they feel so fresh. I think most of us gravitate toward one season or another because we like certain colors or are influenced by the climate or landscape in which we live. The style of our home and furnishings can also dictate which season we prefer when it comes to decorating. There isn't a right or wrong answer here. When you recognize the canvas of your home's primary style, it's just that much easier to add perfectly suited touches later.

To create a space that reflects a season, nothing fancy is required. Just involve all of your senses and celebrate a season's signature scents, sounds, flavors, and looks.

FALL

- Use cinnamon, orange, and clove scents in essential oil diffusers.

- Decorate with leaves, pumpkins, colorful gourds, and pine cones.

- Add more throw blankets and cozy pillows to the chairs and sofas.

- Stock up on books and board games or pull out old favorites for evenings spent indoors.

WINTER

- Drape wreaths, ornaments, and lights on doors, beds, and mirrors. (Now is the time to go crazy with the fairy lights and candles!)

- Add pine cones, mini trees, and evergreen branches to your décor.

- Does the classic red-and-green combo clash with your existing décor? Substitute wintery blues, silvers, and off-whites. A touch of pale pink adds a bit of festivity.

- Think simple and vintage—popcorn and cranberries on the tree, a wooden sled leaning against the front porch, paper snowflakes on the windows.

SPRING

- Lighten up the bedding with fresh white or floral print cotton sheets and soft blankets.

- Display flowers everywhere—tulips, lilacs, daffodils, bluebells. Plant flowers outdoors in hanging baskets, wooden crates, or old metal buckets.

- Dress up the dining room table with springy dishes and patterned cloth napkins.

- Display bowls of colorful fruit in the kitchen and dining room.

SUMMER

- Showcase seaside treasures—starfish, sand dollars, shells, glass containers of sand and pebbles.

- Roll up winter rugs. Expose your bare wood floors or change to cotton rugs in summery stripes and hues.

- Bring out your summer accessories—floral prints, nautical décor, anything that says "summer."

- String fairy lights outdoors along with vibrant paper lanterns to move your living space outdoors.

Is There Victory After (Multiple) Décor Fails?

Yikes—I've really made some decorating blunders! I don't want to lose heart, but how do I not throw in the towel? I'm just not sure I have what it takes!

Christine J.

KariAnne says...

It can be hard to have confidence when you're not certain you're doing something right. And in this day and age of social media and anything and everything is posted for the whole world to see, that confidence is even harder to come by. And some of these images? Well, you just wonder. But hey, I've given them a thumbs-up or a heart anyway. Like the picture of the woman weaving linen for her beach house windows. Or the mom growing her own grain for fresh herb bread for a picnic on a rock at sunset. Yep...

Now, don't get me wrong. I love weaving my own linen as much as the next person. I adore picnics and fresh herb bread. I mean, I'm the one in the grocery line reading about the top ten ways to live healthier and happier for the next five minutes. But let's shift the focus here.

Instead of focusing on someone else's perfection and feeling small when we scroll through all that beautiful, let's stop for a moment. We can feel *less than* when we look at ourselves through the lens of social media. In fact, it's inevitable we will. Those images are cultivated. And edited. With every trick in the book done to them to make them appear perfect. Let's just stop for a moment...and remember how amazing we are.

Sometimes we're in such a mad hurry to make ourselves—and our homes—better. We wish we were living in someone else's house. We wish we had our best friend's decorating budget. Or our favorite blogger's mad skills. Or our neighbor's penchant for organizing and doing everything in a timely manner. But you know what? Someone else is wishing she were you. She's wishing she had your talents and your taste. Really.

So feel free to make mistakes. Paint—and then repaint. Nobody's keeping track. Buy those discount decorations that are calling your name—but keep the receipt. If they don't look right when you get them home, there's no shame in going back to the store and returning them. Go ahead and take a chance at the garage sale. Your DIY project might work—and it might not. But the creative joy is certainly worth a few dollars.

If you have the desire, the imagination, and the inspiration, you have what it takes. And then some. So celebrate YOU—the budding designer, the on-the-way-to-becoming-an-expert decorator, the still-in-process crafter. There's so much beauty in imperfection. You've got this decorating thing. I guarantee it!

About the Authors

Melissa Michaels is a *New York Times* bestselling author and creator of *The Inspired Room*, an award-winning blog that has been one of the top home decorating destinations on the web for more than 11 years. She lives in Seattle with her husband, Jerry; their teen son, Luke; and adorable doodle pups Jack and Lily. The Michaels' two grown daughters, Kylee and Courtney, are a key part of the creative team at *The Inspired Room*.

Connect with Melissa at TheInspiredRoom.net

KariAnne Wood writes the award-winning lifestyle blog Thistlewood Farms, a tiny corner of the internet where all the stories and DIY's hang out and drink sweet tea. She also writes, photographs, and styles for several national magazines including *Better Homes and Gardens*, *Romantic Homes*, *Country Women*, and *Flea Market Décor*. KariAnne is the author of *The DIY Style Finder*, *The DIY Home Planner*, *So Close to Amazing*, and *You've Got This (Because God's Got You)*. This fun-loving mother of four, lives in Dallas with her husband. And don't let her red lipstick fool you—her favorite color is actually gray.

Connect with KariAnne at ThistlewoodFarms.com

For more inspiration and home décor advice, visit

WhereDoIPuttheCouch.com

dwelling

Simple Ways to Nourish
Your Home, Body, & Soul

New York Times Bestselling author
MELISSA MICHAELS
The Inspired Room

THE
Inspired
ROOM

Simple Ideas to
Love the Home You Have

MELISSA
MICHAELS

AUTHOR OF
THE INSPIRED ROOM BLOG

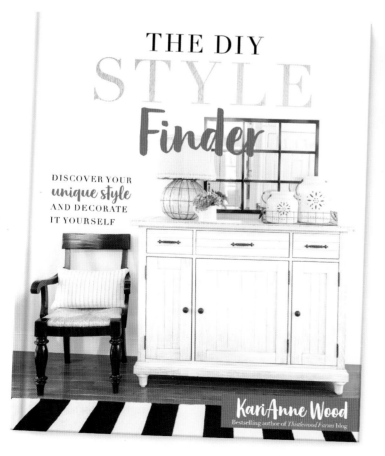

THE DIY
STYLE
Finder

DISCOVER YOUR
unique style
AND DECORATE
IT YOURSELF

KariAnne Wood
Bestselling author of *Thistlewood Farms* blog

THE DIY
Home Planner

Practical Tips & Inspiring Ideas to
DECORATE IT YOURSELF

KARIANNE WOOD
AUTHOR OF THE *THISTLEWOOD FARMS* BLOG
Artwork by Michal Sparks

Cover design by Nicole Dougherty
Interior design by Faceout Studio

Cover images © by poligonchik / Adobe Stock

Published in association with
William K. Jensen Literary Agency,
119 Bampton Court,
Eugene, Oregon 97404

BUT WHERE DO I PUT THE COUCH?
Copyright © 2019 by Melissa Michaels and KariAnne Wood
Published by Harvest House Publishers
Eugene, Oregon 97408
www.harvesthousepublishers.com

ISBN 978-0-7369-7414-1 (Layflat)
ISBN 978-0-7369-7415-8 (eBook)

Library of Congress Cataloging-in-Publication Data

Names: Michaels, Melissa, author. | Wood, KariAnne, author.
Title: But where do I put the couch? / Melissa Michaels and KariAnne Wood.
Description: Eugene, Oregon : Harvest House Publishers, [2019]
Identifiers: LCCN 2018061518 (print) | LCCN 2019000559 (ebook) | ISBN
   9780736974158 (ebook) | ISBN 9780736974141 (pbk.)
Subjects: LCSH: Interior decoration. | House furnishings.
Classification: LCC NK2115 (ebook) | LCC NK2115 .M4588 2019 (print) | DDC
   747--dc23
LC record available at https://lccn.loc.gov/2018061518

Printed in China

19 20 21 22 23 24 25 26 27 / RDS – FO / 10 9 8 7 6 5 4 3 2 1